COOP PREP

Cooperative Admissions Exam
Study Guide and Practice

COMPLETE
Test Preparation Inc.
WWW.TEST-PREPARATION.CA

COPYRIGHT

Copyright © 2025 Complete Test Preparation Inc. ALL RIGHTS RESERVED.

No part of this book may be reproduced or transferred in any form or by any means, graphic, electronic, or mechanical, including photocopying, recording, web distribution, taping, or by any information storage retrieval system, without the written permission of the author.

Notice: Complete Test Preparation Inc. makes every reasonable effort to obtain from reliable sources accurate, complete, and timely information about the tests covered in this book. Nevertheless, changes can be made in the tests or the administration of the tests at any time and Complete Test Preparation Inc. makes no representation or warranty, either expressed or implied as to the accuracy, timeliness, or completeness of the information contained in this book. Complete Test Preparation Inc. makes no representations or warranties of any kind, express or implied, about the completeness, accuracy, reliability, suitability or availability with respect to the information contained in this document for any purpose. Any reliance you place on such information is therefore strictly at your own risk.

The author(s) shall not be liable for any loss incurred as a consequence of the use and application, directly or indirectly, of any information presented in this work. Sold with the understanding, the author is not engaged in rendering professional services or advice. If advice or expert assistance is required, the services of a competent professional should be sought.

The company, product and service names used in this publication are for identification purposes only. All trademarks and registered trademarks are the property of their respective owners. Complete Test Preparation Inc. is not affiliated with any educational institution.

Complete Test Preparation is not affiliated with, or endorsed by any official testing organization. |

All organizational and test names are trademarks of their respective owners.

The makers of the COOP exam are not involved in the production or, and do not endorse this product.

We strongly recommend that students check with exam providers for up-to-date information regarding test content.

ISBN-13: 9781772455106

Version 9 June 2025

About Complete Test Preparation Inc.

Why Us?
The Complete Test Preparation Team has been publishing high quality study materials since 2005, with a catalogue of over 145 titles, in English, French and Chinese, as well as ESL curriculum for all levels.

To keep up with the industry changes, we update everything all the time!

And the best part?
With every purchase, you're helping people all over the world improve themselves and their education. So thank you in advance for supporting this mission with us! Together, we are truly making a difference in the lives of those often forgotten by the system.

Charities that we support
https://www.test-preparation.ca/charities-and-non-profits/

You have definitely come to the right place.
If you want to spend your valuable study time where it will help you the most - we've got you covered today and tomorrow.

Feedback

We welcome your feedback. Email us at feedback@test-preparation.ca with your comments and suggestions. We carefully review all suggestions and often incorporate reader suggestions into upcoming versions. As a Print on Demand Publisher, we update our products frequently.

CONTENTS

6   Getting Started
How this study guide is organized 7
The COOP Study Plan 8
Making a Study Schedule 11

13   Sequences, Analogies & Reasoning
Self-Assessment 17
Answer Key 29
Analogies Tutorial 33
Types of Number Sequence 36
Strategy for Answering Sequence Questions 39
Logic and Reasoning – A Quick Tutorial 40

48   Reading and Language Arts
Self Assessment 51
Answer Key 60
Help with Reading Comprehension 64
Main Idea and Supporting Details 67
Drawing Inferences And Conclusions 71
Meaning From Context 75
English Grammar Self-Assessment 79
English Grammar Multiple Choice 89
Common English Usage Mistakes 107
Subject Verb Agreement 114

120   Mathematics
Self-Assessment 123
Answer Key 135
Fraction Tips, Tricks and Short-cuts 143
Decimal Tips, Tricks and Short-cuts 148
Converting Decimals to Fractions 148
Percent Tips, Tricks and Short-cuts 149
How to Answer Basic Math Questions 151
How to Solve Word Problems 155
Types of Word Problems 158
Basic Algebraic Equations 167
Order of operations 169
Basic Geometry 169
Pythagorean Geometry 174

177 Practice Test Questions Set 1
    Answer Key   232

251 Practice Test Questions Set 2
    Answer Key   302

321 After Taking a Practice Test

325 Online Resources

Getting Started

CONGRATULATIONS! By deciding to take the Cooperative Admissions Exam (COOP), you have taken the first step toward a great future! Of course, there is no point in taking this important examination unless you intend to do your best to earn the highest grade you possibly can. That means getting yourself organized and discovering the best approaches, methods and strategies to master the material. Yes, that will require real effort and dedication on your part, but if you are willing to focus your energy and devote the study time necessary.

We know that taking on a new endeavour can be scary, and it is easy to feel unsure of where to begin. That's where we come in. This study guide is designed to help you improve your test-taking skills, show you a few tricks of the trade and increase both your competency and confidence.

The Cooperative Admissions Exam

The COOP has the following two sections:

Part I - Sequences, Analogies, Quantitative Reasoning and Verbal Reasoning. Each topic has 20 questions and you are given 15 minutes to complete, except analogies where you are given 10 minutes to complete 20 questions.

Part II - Reading and Language Arts, and Math.

Both topics have 40 questions and you are given 40 minutes to complete.

Getting Started

While we seek to make our guide as comprehensive as possible, note that like all entrance exams, the COOP Exam might be adjusted at some future point. New material might be added, or content that is no longer relevant or applicable might be removed. It is always a good idea to give the materials you receive when you register to take the COOP a careful review.

How this study guide is organized

This study guide is divided into three sections. The first section, self-assessments, which will help you recognize your areas of strength and weaknesses. This will be a boon when it comes to managing your study time most efficiently; there is not much point of focusing on material you have already got firmly under control. Instead, taking the self-assessments will show you where that time could be much better spent. In this area you will begin with a few questions to quickly evaluate your understanding of material that is likely to appear on the COOP. If you do poorly in certain areas, simply work carefully through those sections in the tutorials and then try the self-assessment again.

The second section, tutorials, offers information in each of the content areas, as well as strategies to help you master that material. The tutorials are not intended to be a complete course, but cover general principles. If you find that you do not understand the tutorials, it is recommended that you seek out additional instruction.

Third, we offer two sets of practice test questions, similar to those on the COOP Exam.

The COOP Study Plan

Now that you have made the decision to take the COOP, it is time to get started. Before you do another thing, you will need to figure out a plan of attack. The very best study tip is to start early! The longer the time period you devote to regular study practice, the likelier you will be to retain the material and be able to access it quickly. If you thought that 1x20 is the same as 2x10, guess what? It really is not, when it comes to study time. Reviewing material for just an hour per day over the course of 20 days is far better than studying for two hours a day for only 10 days. The more often you revisit a particular piece of information, the better you will know it. Not only will your grasp and understanding be better, but your ability to reach into your brain and quickly and efficiently pull out the tidbit you need, will be greatly enhanced as well.

The great Chinese scholar and philosopher Confucius believed that true knowledge could be defined as knowing what you know and what you do not know. The first step in preparing for the COOP Exam is to assess your strengths and weaknesses. You may already have an idea of what you know and what you do not know, but evaluating yourself using our Self-Assessment modules for each of the areas, Sequences, Analogies, Quantitative Reasoning, Reading Comprehension, Language Arts and Math, will clarify the details.

Making a Study Schedule

To make your study time the most productive, you will need to develop a study plan. The purpose of the plan is to organize all the bits of pieces of information in such a way that you will not feel overwhelmed. Rome was not built in a day, and learning everything you will need to know to pass the COOP Exam is going to take time, too. Arranging the material you need to learn into manageable chunks is the best way to go. Each study session should make you feel as though you have accomplished your goal, or at least are a little closer, and your goal is simply to learn what you planned to learn during that particular session. Try to organize the content in such a way that each study session builds on previous ones. That way, you will retain the information, be better able to access it, and review the previous bits and pieces at the same time.

Self-assessment

The Best Study Tip! The very best study tip is to start early! The longer you study regularly, the more you will retain and 'learn' the material. Studying for 1 hour per day for 20 days is far better than studying for 2 hours for 10 days.

What don't you know?

The first step is to assess your strengths and weaknesses. You may already have an idea of where your weaknesses are, or you can take our Self-assessment modules for each of the areas. Below is a chart with the COOP content areas. Rate each area from one to five. For content that you are very familiar and confident, rate five, and areas that you feel you need to work on, rate one.

Exam Component	Rate 1 to 5
Part I	
Sequences	
Analogies	
Quantitative Reasoning	
Verbal Reasoning (Words)	
Part II	
Verbal Reasoning (In Context)	
Reading & Language Arts	
Sentence Completion	
English Grammar & Usage	
Sentence Combination	
Reading Comprehension	
Mathematics	
Problem Solving (Word Problems)	
Geometry	
Interpreting Data	
Basic Math	

Getting Started

Making a Study Schedule

The key to a successful study plan is to divide the material you need to learn into manageable size and learn it, while at the same time reviewing the material that you already know.

Using the table above, any scores of 3 or below, mean you need to spend time learning, going over, and practicing this subject area. A score of 4 means you need to review the material, but you don't have to spend time re-learning. A score of 5 and you are OK with just an occasional review before the exam.

A score of 0 or 1 means you really need to work on this area and should allocate the most time and the highest priority. Some students prefer a 5-day plan and others a 10-day plan. It also depends on how much time you have until the exam.

Here is an example of a 5-day plan based on an example from the table above:

>**Sequences:** 1 Study 1 hour everyday – review on last day
>**Word Problems:** 3 Study 1 hour for 2 days then ½ hour a day, then review
>**Analogies :** 4 Review every second day
>**English Grammar and Usage:** 2 Study 1 hour on the first day – then ½ hour everyday
>**Reading Comprehension:** 5 Review for ½ hour every other day

Using this example, reading comprehension and analogies are quite good, and only need occasional review. Word problems are pretty good and needs 'some' review. English Grammar needs a bit of work, Sequences need a lot of work and Verbal Analogies are very weak and need the most time. Based on this, here is a sample study plan:

Day	Subject	Time
Monday		
Study	Sequences	1 hour
Study	Word Problems	1 hour
½ hour break		
Study	Grammar	1 hour
Review	Reading Comp.	½ hour
Tuesday		
Study	Sequences	1 hour
Study	Word Problems	½ hour
½ hour break		
Study	Grammar	½ hour
Review	Analogies	½ hour
Review	Usage	½ hour
Wednesday		
Study	Sequences	1 hour
Study	Word Problems	½ hour
½ hour break		
Study	Grammar	½ hour
Review	Reading Comp.	½ hour
Thursday		
Study	Sequences	½ hour
Study	Grammar	½ hour
Review	Vocabulary	½ hour
½ hour break		
Review	Analogies	½ hour
Review	Word Problems	½ hour
Friday		
Review	Sequences	½ hour
Review	Word Problems	½ hour
Review	Grammar	½ hour
½ hour break		
Review	Word Problems	½ hour
Review	Usage	½ hour

Sequences, Analogies and Reasoning

This section contains self-assessments and tutorials for Part I Sequences, Analogies and Quantitative Reasoning. The Tutorials are designed to familiarize general principles and the Self-Assessment contains general questions similar to the questions likely to be on the COOP exam, but are not intended to be identical to the exam questions. The tutorials are not designed to be a complete course, and it is assumed that students have some familiarity with the content. If you do not understand parts of the tutorial, or find the tutorial difficult, it is recommended that you seek out additional instruction.

Note that these questions are for skill practice only. The purpose of the self-assessment is:

- Identify your strengths and weaknesses.
- Develop your personalized study plan (above)
- Get accustomed to the COOP format
- Extra practice – the self-assessments are almost a full 3rd practice test!

Since this is a Self-assessment, and depending on how confident you are with the content, timing is optional. Below is a table with the number of questions and time allowed for each section.

Sequences   20 questions 15 minutes
Analogies   20 questions 7 minutes
Quantitative Reasoning 20 Questions 15 minutes
Verbal Reasoning   20 questions 15 minutes

This self-assessment has 10 of each type, Sequences, Analogies, Quantitative Reasoning and Verbal Reasoning, so allow about 25 minutes to complete the full self-assessment.

The questions below are not the same as you will find on the COOP - that would be too easy! And nobody knows what the questions will be and they change all the time. The questions below cover the same areas as the COOP. So, while the format and exact wording of the questions may differ slightly, and change from year to year, if you can answer the questions below, you will have no problem with the first section of the COOP.

The self-assessment is designed to give you a baseline score in the different areas covered. Here is a brief outline of how your score on the self-assessment relates to your understanding of the material.

75% - 100%	Excellent – you have mastered the content
50 – 75%	Good. You have a working knowledge. Even though you can just pass this section, you may want to review the Tutorials and do some extra practice to see if you can improve your mark.

Analogies, Sequences and Reasoning

25% - 50%	Below Average. You do not understand the material. Review the tutorials, and retake this quiz again in a few days, before proceeding to the rest of the study guide.
Less than 25%	Poor. You have a very limited understanding of the material. Please review the Tutorials, and retake this quiz again in a few days, before proceeding to the rest of the study guide.

After taking the Self-Assessment, use the table above to assess your understanding. If you scored low, read through the tutorials, and make sure you understand everything. Then try again in a few days.

Self-Assessment

	A	B	C	D	E		A	B	C	D	E
1	○	○	○	○	○	21	○	○	○	○	○
2	○	○	○	○	○	22	○	○	○	○	○
3	○	○	○	○	○	23	○	○	○	○	○
4	○	○	○	○	○	24	○	○	○	○	○
5	○	○	○	○	○	25	○	○	○	○	○
6	○	○	○	○	○	26	○	○	○	○	○
7	○	○	○	○	○	27	○	○	○	○	○
8	○	○	○	○	○	28	○	○	○	○	○
9	○	○	○	○	○	29	○	○	○	○	○
10	○	○	○	○	○	30	○	○	○	○	○
11	○	○	○	○	○	31	○	○	○	○	○
12	○	○	○	○	○	32	○	○	○	○	○
13	○	○	○	○	○	33	○	○	○	○	○
14	○	○	○	○	○	34	○	○	○	○	○
15	○	○	○	○	○	35	○	○	○	○	○
16	○	○	○	○	○	36	○	○	○	○	○
17	○	○	○	○	○	37	○	○	○	○	○
18	○	○	○	○	○	38	○	○	○	○	○
19	○	○	○	○	○	39	○	○	○	○	○
20	○	○	○	○	○	40	○	○	○	○	○

Analogies, Sequences and Reasoning 17

Part I - Self-Assessment

Analogies

Directions: Choose the same relationship.

1. **Nest : Bird**
    a. Cave : Bear
    b. Flower : Petal
    c. Window : House
    d. Dog : Basket

2. **Teacher : School**
    a. Businessman : Money
    b. Waitress : Coffee shop
    c. Dentist : Tooth
    d. Fish : Water

3. **Pebble : Boulder**
    a. Pond : Ocean
    a. River: Rapids
    b. Fish : Elephant
    c. Feather : Bird

4. **Poodle : Dog**
    a. Shark : Great White
    b. Dalmatian : Great Dane
    c. Money : Stock Market
    d. Horse : Pony

5. Fox : Chicken

    a. Rat : Mouse

    b. Cat : Mouse

    c. Dog : Cat

    d. Rabbit : Hen

Choose the word that expresses the same concept.

6. Attempt

    a. Persuade

    b. Effort

    c. Endeavor

    d. Perform

7. Authority

    a. Power

    b. Rule

    c. Knowledge

    d. Age

8. Slow : Fast :: Asleep : ___

    a. Awake

    b. Alert

    c. Bright

    d. Sleeping

Analogies, Sequences and Reasoning

9. Lower : Raise :: Complicate : ___

    a. Strengthen

    b. Untangle

    c. Simplify

    d. Solve

10. Expand : Contract :: Accept : ___

    a. Approve

    b. Disprove

    c. Deny

    d. Allow

Sequences Self-Assessment

11. Consider the following sequence: 6, 12, 24, 48, ... What number should come next?

    a. 48

    b. 64

    c. 60

    d. 96

12. Consider the following sequence: 5, 6, 11, 17, ... What number should come next?

    a. 28

    b. 34

    c. 36

    d. 27

13. Consider the following sequence: 26, 21, ..., 11, 6. What is the missing number?

    a. 27

    b. 23

    c. 16

    d. 29

14. Consider the following sequence: L, O, R, ..., Y What is the missing letter?

    a. S

    b. U

    c. T

    d. M

15. Consider the following sequence: X, Z, B, D, ... What number should come next?

    a. E

    b. F

    c. G

    d. H

16. Consider the sequence in row A compared to row B. What is the missing number?

A	5	20	100	3	24
B	20	80	400	12	?

    a. 96

    b. 48

    c. 64

    d. 66

Analogies, Sequences and Reasoning

**17. Consider the following sequence: L, N, P, R, ...
What letter should come next?**

    a. S

    b. T

    c. U

    d. V

18. Consider the following sequence: M, P, S, , Y. What is the missing letter?

    a. V

    b. T

    c. U

    d. X

19. Consider the following sequence:

 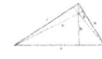 ???

a.  b.  c.

20. Consider the following sequence:

+ * + * | * + * + | * * + * | + + __ __

    a. + *
    b. * *
    c. + +
    d. * +

QUANTITATIVE REASONING SELF-ASSESSMENT

Select the fraction that the shaded area represents.

21.

    a. 1/2
    b. 1/5
    c. 1/4
    d. 1/3

22.

    a. 1/2
    b. 1/5
    c. 1/4
    d. 1/3

Analogies, Sequences and Reasoning

23.

   a. 1/2
   b. 1/5
   c. 1/4
   d. 1/8

24.

   a. 1/2
   b. 1/5
   c. 1/4
   d. 1/8

25. **Which of the following does not belong?**

   a. Abc
   b. bCD
   c. Nmo
   d. Pqr

26. **Which of the following does not belong?**

   a. CD
   b. OP
   c. LM
   d. BD

27. Which of the following does not belong?

　　a. 121212
　　b. 141414
　　c. 151415
　　d. 292929

28. Big Bigger Biggest Small Smaller ____

　　a. Tiny
　　b. Large
　　c. Medium
　　d. Smallest

Directions: For questions 29 - 30 look at the scales showing figures of equal weight. Choose the pair that will also balance the scales.

29.

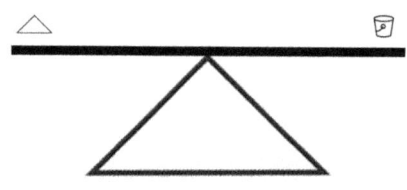

　　a.　△ 🪣　　🪣 🪣
　　b.　△△　　🪣
　　c.　△　　🪣 🪣
　　d.　△ 🪣 🪣　　🪣 🪣

Analogies, Sequences and Reasoning

30.

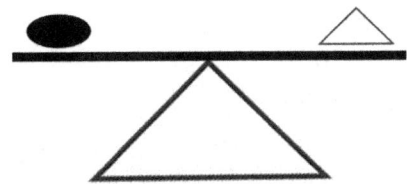

a. ● ●△
b. △△△ ●●
c. △● △△
d. △△ ●

Verbal Reasoning

Find the sentence that is true according to the given information.

31. Britney loves reading books. Susan enjoys playing with her dolls. Britney and Susan are cousins.

    a. Britney likes to play with Susan

    b. Susan finds reading boring

    c. Britney and Susan are blood related

    d. Susan and Britney are best friends

32. The village is found in a coastal area. Many anglers go out to sea everyday. They go home late in the afternoon.

    a. There are many fishers in the village

    b. Many fishermen hate fishing

    c. Fishermen go out to sea especially in the evening

    d. The village attracts tourists

33. Ben and Ted are classmates. They would ride the school bus together. They also have lunch at the same table. They're even lab partners.

    a. Ben and Ted don't like each other

    b. Ben prefers being with other children

    c. Ben and Ted are inseparable

    d. Ted is always alone

34. Karen takes care of her garden everyday. She grows fruits and vegetables. She always waters them. She also pulls out the weeds and put fertilizer on her plants.

    a. Karen hates taking care of her plants

    b. Karen is fond of gardening

    c. Karen plants flowers in her garden

    d. Karen and her mother work on the garden together

Analogies, Sequences and Reasoning

35. Collecting stamps is Tom's hobby. He started collecting stamps when he was six years old. Today, Tom has over a thousand stamps in his collection.

    a. Tom collects stamp albums

    b. Tom started collecting stamps in high school

    c. Tom is a stamp collector

    d. Collecting stamps is an expensive hobby

36. Mother went to market. She bought apples, oranges, and bananas. She also bought cabbage, beans, and squash.

    a. Vegetables in the market are expensive

    b. Mother bought chicken and meat

    c. Many people went to the market

    d. Mother bought fruits and vegetables

37. Which word does not belong with the others?

    a. Jet

    b. Float plane

    c. Kite

    d. Biplane

38. Which of the following does not belong?

    a. Number

    b. Denominate

    c. Numerate

    d. Figure

39. Consider the following sequence: 14, 17, 22, 29, ... What number should come next?

    a. 38
    b. -36
    c. -39
    d. 34

40. Consider the following sequence: 39, 28, 19, 12, 7, ... What number should come next?

    a. 1
    b. 4
    c. 0
    d. 2

Analogies, Sequences and Reasoning

Answer Key

Analogies

1. A
This is a functional relationship. A Bird lives in a nest, the way a bear lives in a cave.

2. B
This is a functional relationship. A teacher works in a school in the same way a waitress works in a coffee shop.

3. A
This is a degree relationship. A boulder is a very large pebble - both are rocks, in the same way that an ocean is a very large pond - both are bodies of water.

4. A
This is a type relationship. A poodle is a type of dog in the same way that a great white is a type of shark.

5. B
This is a predator/prey relationship. Foxes eat chickens in the same way as cats eat mice.

6. B
To attempt is to exert effort or try to achieve something through a set of actions.

7. A
An authority figure is someone who has the power to make rules, persuade, or influence people such as a government official, teacher, or parent.

8. A
This is an antonym relationship. Awake is the antonym of asleep.

9. C

This is an antonym relationship. Simplify is the antonym of complicate.

10. C

This is an antonym relationship. Deny is the antonym of accept.

Sequences Answer Key

11. D

The numbers doubles each time.

12. A

Each number is the sum of the previous two numbers

13. C

The numbers decrease by 5 each time.

14. B

There are two letters missing between each one, so U is next.

15. B

Miss a letter each time and 'loop' back, so F is next.

16. A

The number in row B is 4 times the number in row A.

17. B

One letter is missing after each letter.

18. A

Two letters are missing after each letter.

19. B

The sequence shifts to the left each time, so the next figure will be the circle.

Analogies, Sequences and Reasoning

20. D
Each time the * and + alternate, either singly or doubles.

Quantitative Reasoning

21. C
1 of the 4 divisions is shaded – 1 out of 4 is 1/4.

22. A
2 of the 4 divisions are shaded – 2 out of 4 is equal to 1/2.

23. D
2 of the 16 squares are shaded – 2 out of 16 equals 1/8.

24. C
2 of the 8 sections are shaded – 2 out of 8 equals 1/4.

25. B
This is a capital small letter relationship. All choices start with a capital letter.

26. D
BD is not a sequence of consecutive letters.

27. C
This is a repetition pattern. All the choices repeat a 2-letter sequence except C.

28. D
All the words are comparative adjectives.

29. A
The two figures are equal. Choice A is the only combination where the weights are equal.

30. C
One oval figure equals one triangle, so they are equal. Choice c, two triangles equals one triangle and one cone.

Verbal Reasoning

31. C
The only certain thing is Britney and Susan are related to each other.

32. A
The only certain thing is the villagers rely on fishing to earn money since they live near the ocean.

33. C
The best answer given the choices, is Ben and Ted are inseparable.

34. B
The best answer given the choices, is Karen is fond of gardening.

35. C
The only certain thing is Tom is a stamp collector.

36. D
The only certain thing is mother bought fruits and vegetables.

37. C
A kite is not a type of plane.

38. D
This is a relationship of words question. All the choices are synonyms of count, except figure.

39. A
The first two terms increased by +3. The difference between each subsequent term is the rate of last increase + 2. So answer is 29 + 7 + 2 = 38

40. B
First two terms decreased by 11 and the subsequent terms decreased by subtracting 2 from the last rate of decrease. Answer is 7 −(5-2) = 7-3 =4.

Analogies, Sequences and Reasoning   33

Analogies Tutorial

Analogies can be tricky for anyone, which is why it is important to have strategies to have a better chance of choosing the correct answer. The following analogies strategies will help you solve these tricky problems.

1. The only way to become better at anything is to practice and the same is true for analogies. There really is not any other way to study for verbal analogies than by practicing them.

2. It does not matter how many relationships you can find between the words given in a verbal analogy, what is important is that you give the answer the test-maker is looking for. This strategy is to give the exact answer. Many times, the relationships you think you see are much more in depth than what the test maker is looking for. The following is an example of what this means:

Bigotry/Hatred

    a. sweetness: bitterness

    b. segregation: integration

    c. equality: government

    d. fanaticism: intolerance

You might automatically think that 'bigot' is to 'hate' or that 'bigots hate' is very similar to 'c,' as equality is normally associated with the government or 'd,' and fanatics are often seen as intolerable. The problem is that this way of thinking is subjective or prejudiced and that not everyone thinks like this, so how can those choices be true. You will notice though, that choices 'b,' and 'd,' are not a subjective thought but rather a social extreme, just as 'Bigotry/hatred' is. The way to narrow down the choices more is by looking at the words and their relation to each other, 'bigotry and hatred' are similar terms, but choice 'b,' is not, they are opposite words. 'd,' would be the correct choice because they are also similar terms.

3. Another strategy you can use with verbal analogies is to pick out a word or words that are similar to those in the analogy. This means to find a word that will name the relationship of the given words. The main relationships found in analogies and are listed below:

- **Purpose:** This means that 'A' is used for 'B' the same way that 'X' is used for 'Y'.

- **Cause and Effect:** This means that 'A' has an effect on 'B' the same way that 'X' has an effect on 'Y'.

- **Part to Whole** (individual to group): This means that 'A' is a part of 'B' the same way that 'X' is a part of 'Y'

- **Part to part:** 'A' and 'B' are both parts of something the way that 'X' and 'Y' are both parts of something

- **Action to object:** 'A' is done to 'B' the same way 'X' is done to 'Y'.

- **Object to action:** 'A' does something to 'B' just as 'X' does something to 'Y'.

- **Word meaning:** 'A' means about the same as 'B' and 'X' means about the same as 'Y'

- **Opposite word meaning:** 'A means about the opposite of 'B' and 'X' means about the opposite of 'Y'

- **Sequence:** 'A' comes before (or after) B" just as 'X' comes before (or after) 'Y'.

- **Place:** 'A' and 'B' are related places just as 'X' and 'Y' are related places.

- **Magnitude:** 'A' is greater than (or less than) 'B' and 'X' is greater than (or less than) 'Y'.

Analogies, Sequences and Reasoning   *35*

- **Grammatical:** 'A' and 'B' are parts of speech related to each other-noun to noun, adjective to noun, etc.- in the same way that parts of speech 'X' and 'Y' are related to each other.

4. The next strategy is to read the verbal analogies in sentences. If you take the example above, you could read it something like this 'Bigotry relates to hatred in the same way that'|' and insert each of the choices at the end like 'equality relates to government', etc'. You can change how you word the sentence to whichever relationship is between the words.

5. Sometimes it is difficult to identify the relationship by just looking at the analogy in the order it is represented, so switch the words and try to find a relationship that way. Therefore, instead of considering how 'bigotry' relates to 'hatred' try to see how 'hatred' relates to 'bigotry'. If you are still stuck you can start finding relationships between the first and second word of the given analogy and the first and second word in the choices, respectively, of course. Compare all the first words to the original first word, and the second with the second word.

6. As with all types of tests, you can make an educated guess when all other strategies have failed. Follow your hunches, choose a letter that you have not chosen in a while, or maybe just mark the most complex relationship you see in the choices, if you are pressed for time.

Sequences Tutorial

Answering sequence questions is a skill of recognizing patterns, and the best way to improve is to familiarize yourself with the different types, and to practice. Here is a typical example:

Consider the following series: 26, 21, ..., 11, 6. What is the missing number?

    a. 27

    b. 23

    c. 16

    d. 29

Looking carefully at the sequence, we can see right away that each number is 5 less than the previous number, so the missing number is 16.

We can re-write this sequence in mathematical notation as, a^1, a^2, a^3, ... an, where n is an integer and an is called its nth term. And we can write the sequence in the form of a formula, where an integer is substituted in the place of the variable in the formula and the terms are obtained.

For example, let us consider the sequence 5,10,15,20,...

- Here, $a^n = 5^n$. The formula $a^n = 5^n$.

- The nth term of a sequence can be found by plugging n into the formula for the sequence. So for example, if we wanted to find the 100th number in this sequence, we would substitute n=100 in the formula and get 500.

Types of Number Sequence Problems

1. Simple addition or subtraction – each number in the sequence is obtained by adding a number to the previous number.

For example,   2, 5, 8, 11, 14

Analogies, Sequences and Reasoning

Each number in the sequence is obtained by adding 3 to the previous number, which we could write as, $a^{n+1} = a^n + 3$.

2. Simple multiplication - each number in the sequence is obtained by multiplying the previous number by a whole number or fraction.

For example,   3, 6, 18, 54

Or,

20, 10, 5, 2.5

Each number in the first sequence is obtained by multiplying the previous number by 3, which we could write as, $a^{n+1} = a^n \times 3$.

In the second example, each number in the series is the previous number divided by 2, or multiplied by ½, or $a^{n+1} = a^n \times 1/2$.

3. Prime Numbers – each number in the sequence is a prime number.

For example,

23, ... , 31, 37

Answer: 29

4. Operations on the previous two numbers

For example,

8, 14, 22, 36, 58

Here the sequence is created by adding the previous 2 numbers.

5. Exponents

The number sequence is created by squaring or cubing each number.

For example,

3, 9, 81, 6561, where each number is squared.

6. Combining Sequences

2, 7, 13, 20, 28, 37

Here the sequence starts with 2, and each element is added to another sequence starting with 5. So, 2 + 5 = 7, 7 + 6 = 13, 13 + 7 = 20 and so on.

A variation is a sequence with a repeating element. For example,

1, 2, 3, 5, 7, 9, 12, 15

Here the sequence is, for each n, +1, +1, +1, +2, +2, +2, +3, +3,

7. Fractions

For example,

16/4, 4/2, 2/2, ½,

Fractions are often meant to confuse. If fractions don't have an obvious relationship, reduce them to lowest terms or to whole numbers. Reducing these to whole numbers, gives,

4, 2, 1, ½

Right away, we can see the numbers are half the previous number, so the next in the series is ¼.

Analogies, Sequences and Reasoning

In this example, the answer is a fraction; however, you may have to reduce fractions to see the relation, and then convert back to get the answer in the correct form.

Strategy for Answering Sequence Questions

Here is a quick method that will help you answer number series.

For example:

2, 5, 6, 7, 8,

Step 1 – glance at the series quickly and see if you can spot the pattern right away.

Step 2 – Start analyzing.

Take the different between the first 2 numbers and the different between the second 2 numbers.

2, (+3) 5, (+1) 6, (+1) 7, (+1) 8,

No clear pattern with a simple analysis. There is no addition, subtraction, multiplication, division, fractional or exponent relationship.

The relation must be a higher order or a second series.

Next look at the relation between the 1st number and the 2nd and the 1st and the 3rd.   We see that,

1st + 3 = 5, 1st + 4 = 6. That's it! The number 2 is added to the sequence, 3, 4, 5, 6, so the next number will be 2 + 7 = 9.

Logic and Reasoning – A Quick Tutorial

Understanding reasoning problems is very tricky so it is important to understand the structure and strategies for solving the problem. Often, once you see the structure, the answer becomes clear immediately. Here are some tips to guide you when reviewing for reasoning, which are derived from syllogisms, exam questions:

Logical syllogisms have three key components: the major premise, minor premise, and the conclusion. Practicing logic questions helps you identify these quickly and easily.

There are two terms used in each part, which can be understood through the form ""Some/all A is/are [not] B." Each premise has a common term with the conclusion as seen in the example below:

Premise: All birds are animals

Premise: All parrots are birds

Conclusion: All parrots are animals

In this example, "animal" is the major term and predicate of the conclusion, "parrot" is the minor term and subject of the conclusion, and "bird" is the middle term.

Clearly, this argument is rock-solid. If ALL birds are animals, AND all parrots are birds, then the conclusion, All parrots must be animals, must be true.

To check this, let's try a variation:

Some birds are animals.

All parrots are birds

All parrots are animals.

Clearly, this is not true. If only 'some' birds are animals, then there are some birds which are NOT animals, and we don't have any information about the 'some' birds which are not animals. Perhaps the "some birds" that are not animals are parrots, and perhaps not.

Analogies, Sequences and Reasoning

Here is another example:

> This store only sells used textbooks.
> My textbook is used.
> My textbook came from that store.

This is clearly a not true. We do not know if the store is the only store in the world that sells textbooks, so clearly the textbook in question could have come from that store or any other store.

Structure

There are four possible variations to each "Some/all/no A is/are [not] B," structure.

> All birds are animals.
> All parrots are birds.
> All parrots are animals.

Clearly a very solid argument – IF all birds are animals, AND all parrots are birds, then the conclusion, all parrots are animals MUST be true.

Here is a variation that is NOT true:

> Some birds are animals.
> All parrots are birds.
> All parrots are animals.

Here we don't know if the 'some' birds that are NOT animals includes parrots or not. They may be but we do not know.

Here is the negative example:

> No birds are foxes.
> All parrots are birds.
> No parrots are foxes.

A very good argument where the conclusion, No parrots are foxes MUST be true if the premises are true.

Notice what happens if we substitute 'some' into the argument.

> Some birds are foxes.
> All parrots are birds.
> No parrots are foxes.

> No birds are foxes.
> Some parrots are birds.
> No parrots are foxes.

Both of these are clearly false. The argument relies on the absolute statements ALL and NONE in the first premise.

Using some can give a very solid argument though. Consider these:

> All dogs are animals.
> Some mammals are dogs.
> Some mammals are animals.

> No dogs are birds.
> Some mammals are dogs.
> Some mammals are not birds.

> No restaurant food is healthy.
> Some recipes are healthy.
> Some recipes are not restaurant foods.

> All liars are evildoers.
> Some doctors are not evildoers.
> Some doctors are not liars.

Analogies, Sequences and Reasoning

All these are very good arguments where the conclusion MUST be true if the premises are true.

At the end of this section is a comprehensive list of all valid logic argument forms. Study these forms and make sure that you are familiar with them and understand why the conclusion must be true.

The Real World

Generally, exam questions are not exactly like the forms we have been discussing so far, but are similar. Understanding the correct forms is still very important and necessary to understand the underlying structure.

Here are some example logic questions:

> 1. Practice makes perfect.
> I am perfect.
> I practiced a lot.

If the first 2 statements are true, then the third statement is:

A. True   B. False   C. Uncertain

The correct answer is - Uncertain. There are all sorts of reasons you could be perfect without practicing. For example, you could be perfect looking, or your hair could be perfect.

> 2. People who smoke cigarettes have a 75% chance of getting cancer.
> I have cancer.
> I smoked a lot.

If the first 2 statements are true, then the third statement is:

A. True   B. False   C. Uncertain

The correct answer is - Uncertain. There are many reasons

you could have cancer. In addition, you may be among the 25% of people who smoke and do not get cancer.

    3. Most car accidents happen in the morning.
    I don't drive in the morning.
    I am unlikely to have an accident.

If the first 2 statements are true, then the third statement is:

A. True   B. False   C. Uncertain

The correct answer is - Uncertain. It is possible that you could have an accident driving in the morning, since that is when most accidents occur, however, it is possible that you will not also.

    4. Halibut are a large fish.
    I caught a small fish.
    I did not catch a halibut.

If the first 2 statements are true, then the third statement is:

A. True   B. False   C. Uncertain

The correct answer is – False. You could have caught a baby halibut. In order for this to be true, you would have to say,

All halibut are large fish.
I caught a small fish.
I did not catch a halibut.

Here, the first premise is ALL halibut are large, which would include baby halibut, so if the first two premises are true, the third statement MUST be true also.

Analogies, Sequences and Reasoning

A Different Style

Here is a different style of question similar to what you will find on the COOP.

1. Angel gets the highest grades in all the subjects in school. She is also the president of the Student Council. Every year she gets the highest award given by the school.

    a. Angel is a slow learner.

    b. Everybody admires Angel.

    c. Other children are envious of Angel.

    d. Angel is at the top of her class.

Let's look at the choices. Option a. is clearly false. Option b, may be true but it also may not be true – no information is given. It is likely that everyone admires her, but we don't know that for sure. The same with option c. Probably other students are envious of her, but we don't know that for sure and no information is given. She could, for example, have rigged the election for Student Council and cheated on all her exams and everyone hates her!

Option d. is correct – This we do now for sure.

2. Students enjoy playing football after school. Sometimes, they play basketball with other kids. On weekends, they play baseball, badminton, or tennis.

    a. Students prefer playing indoors.

    b. Students enjoy different kinds of sports.

    c. Students hate playing.

    d. Playing is a form of exercise.

The correct answer is b. The only certain thing is children enjoy different kinds of sports. For option a., no information is given if they are playing indoors or outdoors. Option c. is probably false, but we don't know. Option d. is true, but not related to the information given. Option d. is designed to confuse.

List of all Valid Logic Argument forms

All men are fallible.
All men are animals.
Some animals are fallible.

Some books are precious.
All books are perishable.
Some perishable things are precious.

All books are imperfect.
Some books are informative.
Some informative things are imperfect.

No snakes are good to eat.
All snakes are animals.
Some animals are not good to eat.

Some websites are not helpful.
All websites are internet resources.
Some internet resources are not helpful.

No lepers are allowed to enter the church.
All lepers are human.
Some humans are not allowed to enter the church.

All pigs are unclean.
All unclean things are best avoided.

Analogies, Sequences and Reasoning

Some things that are best avoided are pigs.

All trees are plants.
No plants are birds.
No birds are trees.

Some evil doers are lawyers.
All lawyers are human.
Some humans are evil doers.

No meals are free.
All free things are desirable.
Some desirable things are not meals.

No dogs are birds.
Some birds are pets.
Some pets are not dogs.

Reading and Language Arts

This Section Contains a self-assessment and Reading Comprehension tutorials. The Tutorials are designed to familiarize general principles and the Self-Assessment contains general questions similar to the questions likely to be on the COOP exam, but are not intended to be identical to the exam questions. The tutorial is not designed to be a complete course, and it is assumed that students have some familiarity with reading comprehension. If you do not understand parts of the tutorial, or find the tutorial difficult, it is recommended that you seek out additional instruction.

Note that these questions are for skill practice only. The purpose of the self-assessment is:

- Identify your strengths and weaknesses.

- Develop your personalized study plan (above)

- Get accustomed to the COOP format

- Extra practice – the self-assessments are almost a full 3rd practice test!

Since this is a Self-assessment, and depending on how confident you are with Reading Comprehension, timing is optional. The COOP has 40 reading comprehension and language arts questions combined, to be answered in 40 minutes. The reading comprehension self-assessment below has 12 questions, so allow about 12 minutes to complete this assessment.

Reading and Language Arts

The questions below are not the same as you will find on the COOP - that would be too easy! And nobody knows what the questions will be and they change all the time. Below are general Reading Comprehension questions that cover the same areas as the COOP. So, while the format and exact wording of the questions may differ slightly, and change from year to year, if you can answer the questions below, you will have no problem with the Reading Comprehension section of the COOP.

The self-assessment is designed to give you a baseline score in the different areas covered. Here is a brief outline of how your score on the self-assessment relates to your understanding of the material.

75% - 100%	Excellent – you have mastered the content
50 – 75%	Good. You have a working knowledge. Even though you can just pass this section, you may want to review the Tutorials and do some extra practice to see if you can improve your mark.
25% - 50%	Below Average. You do not understand reading comprehension problems. Review the tutorials, and retake this quiz again in a few days, before proceeding to the rest of the study guide.
Less than 25%	Poor. You have a very limited understanding of the reading comprehension problems. Please review the Tutorials, and retake this quiz again in a few days, before proceeding to the rest of the study guide.

Reading Comprehension

	A	B	C	D
1	○	○	○	○
2	○	○	○	○
3	○	○	○	○
4	○	○	○	○
5	○	○	○	○
6	○	○	○	○
7	○	○	○	○
8	○	○	○	○
9	○	○	○	○
10	○	○	○	○
11	○	○	○	○
12	○	○	○	○
13	○	○	○	○
14	○	○	○	○
15	○	○	○	○
16	○	○	○	○

Reading and Language Arts

Directions: The following questions are based on several reading passages. A series of questions follow each passage. Read each passage carefully, and then answer the questions based on it. You may reread the passage as often as you wish. When you have finished answering the questions based on one passage, go right onto the next passage. Choose the best answer based on the information given and implied.

Questions 1 – 4 refer to the following passage.

Passage 1 - Who Was Anne Frank?

You may have heard mention of the word Holocaust in your History or English classes. The Holocaust took place from 1939-1945. It was an attempt by the Nazi party to purify the human race, by eliminating Jews, Gypsies, Catholics, homosexuals and others they deemed inferior to their "perfect" Aryan race. The Nazis used Concentration Camps, which were sometimes used as Death Camps, to exterminate the people they held in the camps. The saddest fact about the Holocaust was the over one million children under the age of sixteen died in a Nazi concentration camp. Just a few weeks before World War II was over, Anne Frank was one of those children to die.

Before the Nazi party began its persecution of the Jews, Anne Frank had a happy live. She was born in June of 1929. In June of 1942, for her 13th birthday, she was given a simple present which would go onto impact the lives of millions of people around the world. That gift was a small red diary that she called Kitty. This diary was to become Anne's most treasured possession when she and her family hid from the Nazi's in a secret annex above her father's office building in Amsterdam.

For 25 months, Anne, her sister Margot, her parents, another family, and an elderly Jewish dentist hid from the Nazis in this tiny annex. They were never permitted to go outside, and their food and supplies were brought to them by Miep Gies and her husband, who did not believe in the

Nazi persecution of the Jews. It was a very difficult life for young Anne and she used Kitty as an outlet to describe her life in hiding.

After 2 years, Anne and her family were betrayed and arrested by the Nazis. To this day, nobody is exactly sure who betrayed the Frank family and the other annex residents. Anne, her mother, and her sister were separated from Otto Frank, Anne's father. Then, Anne and Margot were separated from their mother. In March of 1945, Margot Frank died of starvation in a Concentration Camp. A few days later, at the age of 15, Anne Frank died of typhus. Of all the people who hid in the Annex, only Otto Frank survived the Holocaust.

Otto Frank returned to the Annex after World War II. It was there that he found Kitty, filled with Anne's thoughts and feelings about being a persecuted Jewish girl. Otto Frank had Anne's diary published in 1947 and it has remained continuously in print ever since. Today, the diary has been published in over 55 languages and more than 24 million copies have been sold around the world. The Diary of Anne Frank tells the story of a brave young woman who tried to see the good in all people.

1. From the context clues in the passage, what does annex mean?

    a. Attic

    b. Bedroom

    c. Basement

    d. Kitchen

Reading and Language Arts 53

2. Why do you think Anne's diary has been published in 55 languages?

    a. So everyone could understand it.

    b. So people around the world could learn more about the horrors of the Holocaust.

    c. Because Anne was Jewish but hid in Amsterdam and died in Germany.

    d. Because Otto Frank spoke many languages.

3. From the description of Anne and Margot's deaths in the passage, what can we assume typhus is?

    a. The same as starving to death.

    b. An infection the Germans gave to Anne.

    c. A disease Anne caught in the concentration camp.

    d. Poison gas used by the Germans to kill Anne.

4. In the third paragraph, what does outlet mean?

    a. A place to plug things into the wall

    b. A store where Miep bought cheap supplies for the Frank family

    c. A hiding space similar to an Annex

    d. A place where Anne could express her private thoughts.

Questions 5 – 8 refer to the following passage.

Passage 2 - Was Dr. Seuss a Real Doctor?

A favorite author for over 100 years, Theodor Seuss Geisel was born on March 2, 1902. Today, we celebrate the birthday of the famous "Dr. Seuss" by hosting Read Across America events throughout the March. School children around the country celebrate the "Doctor's" birthday by making hats, giving presentations and holding read aloud circles featuring some of Dr. Seuss' most famous books.

But who was Dr. Seuss? Did he go to medical school? Where was his office? You may be surprised to know that Theodor Seuss Geisel was not a medical doctor at all. He took on the nickname Dr. Seuss when he became a noted children's book author. He earned the nickname because people said his books were "as good as medicine." All these years later, his nickname has lasted and he is known as Dr. Seuss all across the world.

Think back to when you were a young child. Did you ever want to try "green eggs and ham?" Did you try to "Hop on Pop?" Do you remember learning about the environment from a creature called The Lorax? Of course, you must recall one of Seuss' most famous characters; that green Grinch who stole Christmas. These stories were all written by Dr. Seuss and featured his signature rhyming words and letters. They also featured made up words to enhance his rhyme scheme and even though many of his characters were made up, they sure seem real to us today.

And what of his "signature" book, The Cat in the Hat? You must remember that cat and Thing One and Thing Two from your childhood. Did you know that in the early 1950's there was a growing concern in America that children were not becoming avid readers? This was, book publishers thought, because children found books dull and uninteresting. An intelligent publisher sent Dr. Seuss a book of words that he thought all children should learn as young readers. Dr. Seuss wrote his famous story The Cat in the Hat, using those words. We can see, over the decades, just how much influence his writing has had on very young children. That is why we celebrate this doctor's birthday each March.

5. What does the word "avid" mean in the last paragraph?

  a. Good

  b. Interested

  c. Slow

  d. Fast

6. What can we infer from the statement " His books were like medicine?"

    a. His books made people feel better

    b. His books were in doctor's office waiting rooms

    c. His books took away fevers

    d. His books left a funny taste in readers' mouths.

7. Why is the publisher in the last paragraph called "intelligent?"

    e. a. The publisher knew how to read.

    b. The publisher knew that kids did not like to read.

    c. The publisher knew Dr. Seuss would be able to create a book that sold well.

    d. The publisher knew that Dr. Seuss would be able to write a book that would get young children interested in reading.

8. The theme of this passage is

    a. Dr. Seuss was not a doctor.

    b. Dr. Seuss influenced the lives of generations of young children.

    c. Dr. Seuss wrote rhyming books.

    d. Dr. Suess' birthday is a good day to read a book.

Questions 9 - 12 refer to the following passage.

Keeping Tropical Fish

Keeping tropical fish at home or in your office used to be very popular. Today, interest has declined, but it remains as rewarding and relaxing a hobby as ever. Ask any tropical fish hobbyist, and you will hear how soothing and relaxing watching colorful fish live their lives in the aquarium. If you are considering keeping tropical fish as pets, here is a list of the basic equipment you will need.

A filter is essential for keeping your aquarium clean and your fish alive and healthy. There are different types and sizes of filters and the right size for you depends on the size of the aquarium and the level of stocking. Generally, you need a filter with a 3 to 5 times turn over rate per hour. This means that the water in the tank should go through the filter about 3 to 5 times per hour.

Most tropical fish do well in water temperatures ranging between 24° C and 26° C, though each has its own ideal water temperature. A heater with a thermostat is necessary to regulate the water temperature. Some heaters are submersible and others are not, so check carefully before you buy.

Lights are also necessary, and come in a large variety of types, strengths and sizes. A light source is necessary for plants in the tank to photosynthesize and give the tank a more attractive appearance. Even if you plan to use plastic plants, the fish still require light, although here you can use a lower strength light source.

A hood is necessary to keep dust, dirt and unwanted materials out of the tank. Sometimes the hood can also help prevent evaporation. Another requirement is aquarium gravel. This will improve the aesthetics of the aquarium and is necessary if you plan to have real plants.

9. What is the general tone of this article?

    a. Formal

    b. Informal

    c. Technical

    d. Opinion

10. Which of the following cannot be inferred?

 a. Gravel is good for aquarium plants.

 b. Fewer people have aquariums in their office than at home.

 c. The larger the tank, the larger the filter required.

 d. None of the above.

11. What evidence does the author provide to support their claim that aquarium lights are necessary?

 a. Plants require light.

 b. Fish and plants require light.

 c. The author does not provide evidence for this statement.

 d. Aquarium lights make the aquarium more attractive.

12. Which of the following is an opinion?

 a. Filter with a 3 to 5 times turn over rate per hour are required.

 b. Aquarium gravel improves the aesthetics of the aquarium.

 c. An aquarium hood keeps dust, dirt and unwanted materials out of the tank.

 d. Each type of tropical fish has its own ideal water temperature.

Questions 13 - 16 refer to the following passage.

The Civil War

The Civil War began on April 12, 1861. The first shots of the Civil War were fired in Fort Sumter, South Carolina. Note that even though more American lives were lost in the Civil War than in any other war, not one person died on that first day. The war began because eleven Southern states seceded from the Union and tried to start their own government, The Confederate States of America.

Why did the states secede? The issue of slavery was a primary cause of the Civil War. The eleven southern states relied heavily on their slaves to foster their farming and plantation lifestyles. The northern states, many of whom had already abolished slavery, did not feel that the southern states should have slaves. The north wanted to free all the slaves and President Lincoln's goal was to both end slavery and preserve the Union. He had Congress declare war on the Confederacy on April 14, 1862. For four long, blood soaked years, the North and South fought.

From 1861 to mid 1863, it seemed as if the South would win this war. However, on July 1, 1863, an epic three day battle was waged on a field in Gettysburg, Pennsylvania. Gettysburg is remembered for being the bloodiest battle in American history. At the end of the three days, the North turned the tide of the war in their favor. The North then went on to dominate the South for the remainder of the war. A famous episode is General Sherman's "March to The Sea," where he famously led the Union Army through Georgia and the Carolinas, burning and destroying everything in their path.
In 1865, the Union army invaded and captured the Confederate capital of Richmond Virginia. Robert E. Lee, leader of the Confederacy surrendered to General Ulysses S. Grant, leader of the Union forces, on April 9, 1865. The Civil War was over and the Union was preserved.

13. What does secede mean?

    a. To break away from

    b. To accomplish

    c. To join

    d. To lose

Reading and Language Arts

14. Which of the following statements summarizes a FACT from the passage?

    a. Congress declared war and then the Battle of Fort Sumter began.

    b. Congress declared war after shots were fired at Fort Sumter.

    c. President Lincoln was pro slavery

    d. President Lincoln was at Fort Sumter with Congress

15. Which event finally led the Confederacy to surrender?

    a. The battle of Gettysburg

    b. The battle of Bull Run

    c. The invasion of the confederate capital of Richmond

    d. Sherman's March to the Sea

16. What does the word abolish as used in this passage mean?

    a. To ban

    b. To polish

    c. To support

    d. To destroy

Answer Key

1. A
We know that an annex is like an attic because the text states the annex was above Otto Frank's building.

Choice B is incorrect because an office building doesn't have bedrooms. Choice C is incorrect because a basement would be below the office building. Choice D is incorrect because there would not be a kitchen in an office building.

2. B
The diary has been published in 55 languages so people all over the world can learn about Anne. That is why the passage says it has been continuously in print.

Choice A is incorrect because it is too vague. Choice C is incorrect because it was published after Anne died and she did not write in all three languages. Choice D is incorrect because the passage does not give us any information about what languages Otto Frank spoke.

3. C
Use the process of elimination to figure this out.

Choice A cannot be the correct answer because otherwise the passage would have simply said that Anne and Margot both died of starvation. Choices B and D cannot be correct because if the Germans had done something specifically to murder Anne, the passage would have stated that directly. By the process of elimination, choice C has to be the correct answer.

4. D
We can figure this out using context clues. The paragraph is talking about Anne's diary and so, outlet in this instance is a place where Anne can pour her feelings.

Choice A is incorrect answer. That is the literal meaning of the word outlet and the passage is using the figurative meaning. Choice B is incorrect because that is the secondary literal meaning of the word outlet, as in an outlet mall.

Reading and Language Arts

Again, we are looking for figurative meaning. Choice C is incorrect because there are no clues in the text to support that answer.

5. B
When someone is avid about something that means they are highly interested in the subject. The context clues are dull and boring, because they define the opposite of avid.

6. A
The author is using a simile to compare the books to medicine. Medicine is what you take when you want to feel better. They are suggesting that if a person wants to feel good, they should read Dr. Seuss' books.

Choice B is incorrect because there is no mention of a doctor's office. Choice C is incorrect because it is using the literal meaning of medicine and the author is using medicine in a figurative way. Choice D is incorrect because it makes no sense. We know not to eat books.

7. D
The publisher is described as intelligent because he knew to get in touch with a famous author to develop a book that children would be interested in reading.

Choice A is incorrect because we can assume that all book publishers must know how to read. Choice B is incorrect because it says in the article that more than one publisher was concerned about whether or not children liked to read. Choice C is incorrect because there is no mention in the article about how well The Cat in the Hat sold when it was first published.

8. B
The passage describes in detail how Dr. Seuss had a great effect on the lives of children through his writing. It names several of his books, tells how he helped children become avid readers and explains his style of writing.

Choice A is incorrect because that is just one single fact about the passage. Choice C is incorrect because that is just one single fact about the passage. Choice D is incorrect because that is just one single fact about the passage.

Again, choice B is correct because it encompasses ALL the facts in the passage, not just one single fact.

9. B
The general tone is informal.

10. B
The statement, "Fewer people have aquariums in their office than at home," cannot be inferred from this article.

11. B
Light is necessary for the fish and plants.

12. B
The following statement is an opinion, " Aquarium gravel improves the aesthetics of the aquarium."

13. A
Secede means to break away from because the 11 states wanted to leave the United States and form their own country.

Choice B is incorrect because the states were not accomplishing anything. Choice C is incorrect because the states were trying to leave the USA not join it. Choice D is incorrect because the states seceded before they lost the war.

14. B
Look at the dates in the passage. The shots were fired on April 12 and Congress declared war on April 14.

Choice C is incorrect because the passage states that Lincoln was against slavery. Choice D is incorrect because it never mentions who was or was not at Fort Sumter.

15. C
The passage states that Lee surrendered to Grant after the capture of the capital of the Confederacy, which is Richmond.

Choice A is incorrect because the war continued for 2 years after Gettysburg. Choice B is incorrect because that battle is not mentioned in the passage. Choice D is incorrect because the capture of the capital occurred after the march to the sea.

16. A
When the passage said that the North had *abolished* slavery, it implies that slaves were no longer allowed in the North. In essence slavery was banned.

Choice B makes no sense relative to the context of the passage. Choice C is incorrect because we know the North was fighting slavery, not for it. Choice D is incorrect because slavery is not a tangible thing that can be destroyed. It is a practice that had to be outlawed or banned.

Help with Reading Comprehension

At first sight, reading comprehension tests look challenging especially if you are given long essays to answer only two to three questions. While reading, you might notice your attention wandering, or you may feel sleepy. Do not be discouraged because there are various tactics and long-range strategies that make comprehending even long, boring essays easier.

Your friends before your foes. It is always best to start with passages with familiar subjects rather than those with unfamiliar ones. This approach applies the same logic as tackling easy questions before hard ones. Skip passages that do not interest you and leave them for later.

Don't use 'special' reading techniques. This is not the time for speed-reading or anything like that – just plain ordinary reading – not too slow and not too fast.

Read through the entire passage and the questions before you do anything. Many students try reading the questions first and then looking for answers in the passage thinking this approach is more efficient. What these students do not realize is that it is often hard to navigate in unfamiliar roads. If you do not familiarize yourself with the passage first, looking for answers become not only time-consuming but also dangerous because you might miss the context of the answer you are looking for. If you read the questions first you will only confuse yourself and lose valuable time.

Familiarize yourself with reading comprehension questions. If you are familiar with the common types of reading questions, you are able to take note of important parts of the passage, saving time. There are six major kinds of reading questions.

- **Main Idea**- Questions that ask for the central thought or significance of the passage.

- **Specific Details** - Questions that asks for explicitly stated ideas.

Reading and Language Arts

- **Drawing Inferences** - Questions that ask for a logical extension of statements.

- **Tone or Attitude** - Questions that test your ability to sense the emotional state of the author.

- **Context Meaning** – Questions that ask for the meaning of a word depending on the context.

- **Technique** – Questions that ask for the method of organization or the writing style of the author.

Read. Read. Read. The best preparation for reading comprehension tests is always to read, read and read. If you are not used to reading lengthy passages, you will probably lose concentration. Increase your attention span by making a habit out of reading. Read everyday and increase the time slowly each day.

Reading Comprehension tests become less daunting when you have trained yourself to read and understand fast. Always remember that it is easier to understand passages you are interested in. Do not read through passages hastily. Make mental notes of ideas you may be asked.

Reading Strategy

When facing the reading comprehension section of a standardized test, you need a strategy to be successful. You want to keep several steps in mind:

- **First, make a note of the time and the number of sections.** Time your work accordingly. Typically, four to five minutes per section is sufficient. Second, read the directions for each selection thoroughly before beginning (and listen carefully to any additional verbal instructions, as they will often clarify obscure or confusing written guidelines). You must know exactly how to do what you're about to do!

- **Now you're ready to begin reading the selection.** Read the passage carefully, noting significant characters or events on scrap paper or underlining on the test sheet. Many students find making a basic list in the margins helpful. Quickly jot down or underline one-word summaries of characters, notable happenings, numbers, or key ideas. This will help retain information and focus wandering thoughts. Remember, however, that your goal is to find the information that answers the questions. Even if you find the passage interesting, stay on track.

- **Now read the question and all the choices.** Now you have read the passage, have a general idea of the main ideas, and have marked the important points. Read the question and all the choices. Never choose an answer without reading them all! Questions are often designed to confuse – stay focussed and clear. Usually the answer choices will focus on one or two facts or inferences from the passage. Keep these clear in your mind.

- **Search for the answer.** With a very general idea of what the different choices are, go back to the passage and scan for the relevant information. Watch for big words, unusual or unique words. These make your job easier as you can scan the text for the particular word.

- **Mark the Answer.** Now you have the key information the question is looking for. Go back to the question, quickly scan the choices and mark the correct one.

Typically, there will be several questions dealing with facts from the selection, a couple more inference questions dealing with logical consequences of those facts, and periodically an application-oriented question surfaces to force you to make connections with what you already know. Some students prefer to answer the questions as listed, and feel classifying the question and then ordering is wasting precious time. Other students prefer to answer the different types of questions in order of how easy or difficult they are. The choice is yours and do whatever works for you. If you want to try answering in order of difficulty, here is a recommended order, answer fact questions first; they're easily found within the passage. Tackle inference problems next, after re-reading the question(s) as many times as you need to. Application or 'best guess' questions usually take the longest, so, save them for last.

Use the practice tests to try out both ways of answering and see what works for you.

For more help with reading comprehension, see Multiple Choice Secrets at www.multiple-choice.ca

Main Idea and Supporting Details

Identifying the main idea, topic and supporting details in a passage can feel like an overwhelming task. The passages used for standardized tests can be boring and seem difficult - Test writers don't use interesting passages or ones that talk about things most people are familiar with. Despite these obstacles, all passages and paragraphs will have the information you need to answer the questions.

The topic of a passage or paragraph is its subject. It's the general idea and can be summed up in a word or short phrase. Sometimes, there is a short description of the passage if it's taken from a longer work. Make sure you read the description as it might state the topic of the passage. If not, read the passage and ask yourself, "Who, or what is this about?" For example:

> Over the years, school uniforms have been hotly debated. Arguments are made that students have the right to show individuality and express themselves by choosing their own clothes. However, this brings up social and academic issues. Some kids cannot af-

ford to wear the clothes they like and might be bullied by the "better dressed" students. With attention drawn to clothes and the individual, students will lose focus on class work and the reason they are in school. School uniforms should be mandatory.

Ask: What is this paragraph about?

Topic: school uniforms

Once you have the topic, it's easier to find the main idea. The main idea is a specific statement telling what the writer wants you to know. Writers usually state the main idea as a thesis statement. If you're looking for the main idea of a single paragraph, the main idea is called the topic sentence and will probably be the first or last sentence. If you're looking for the main idea of an entire passage, look for the thesis statement in either the first or last paragraph. The main idea is usually restated in the conclusion. To find the main idea of a passage or paragraph, follow these steps:

1. Find the topic.

2. Ask yourself, "What point is the author trying to make about the topic?"

3. Create your own sentence summarizing the author's point.

4. Look in the text for the sentence closest in meaning to yours.

Look at the example paragraph again. It's already established that the topic of the paragraph is school uniforms. What is the main idea/topic sentence?

Ask: "What point is the author trying to make about school uniforms?"

Summary: Students should wear school uniforms.

Topic sentence: School uniforms should be mandatory.

Reading and Language Arts

Main Idea: School uniforms should be mandatory.

Each paragraph offers supporting details to explain the main idea. The details could be facts or reasons, but they will always answer a question about the main idea. What? Where? Why? When? How? How much/many? Look at the example paragraph again. You'll notice that more than one sentence answers a question about the main idea. These are the supporting details.

Main Idea: School uniforms should be mandatory.

Ask: Why? Some kids cannot afford to wear clothes they like and could be bullied by the "better dressed" kids. Supporting Detail

With attention drawn to clothes and the individual, Students will lose focus on class work and the reason they are in school. Supporting Detail

What if the author doesn't state the main idea in a topic sentence? The passage will have an implied main idea. It's not as difficult to find as it might seem. Paragraphs are always organized around ideas. To find an implied main idea, you need to know the topic and then find the relationship between the supporting details. Ask yourself, "What is the point the author is making about the relationship between the details?"

> Cocoa is what makes chocolate good for you. Chocolate comes in many varieties. These delectable flavors include milk chocolate, dark chocolate, semi-sweet, and white chocolate.

Ask: What is this paragraph about?

Topic: Chocolate

Ask: What? Where? Why? When? How? How much/many?

Supporting details: Chocolate is good for you because it is made of cocoa, Chocolate is delicious, Chocolate comes in different delicious flavors

Ask: What is the relationship between the details and what is the author's point?

Main Idea: Chocolate is good because it is healthy and it tastes good.

Testing Tips for Main Idea Questions

1. Skim the questions – not the answer choices - before reading the passage.

2. Questions about main idea might use the words "theme," "generalization," or "purpose."

3. Save questions about the main idea for last. Questions can often be found in order in the passage.

3. Underline topic sentences in the passage. Most tests allow you to write in your test booklet.

4. Answer the question in your own words before looking at the answer choices. Then match your answer with an answer choice.

5. Cross out incorrect answer choices immediately to prevent confusion.

6. If two of the answer choices mean the same thing but use different words, they are BOTH incorrect.

7. If a question asks about the whole passage, cross out the answer choices that apply to only part of it.

8. If only part of the information is correct, that answer choice is incorrect.

9. An answer choice that is too broad is incorrect. All information needs to be backed up by the passage.

10. Answer choices with extreme wording are usually incorrect.

Reading and Language Arts

Drawing Inferences And Conclusions

Drawing inferences and making conclusions happens all the time. In fact, you probably do it every time you read—sometimes without even realizing it! For example, remember the first time that you saw the movie "The Lion King." When you meet Scar for the first time, he is trapping a helpless mouse with his sharp claws preparing to eat it. When you see this action you guess that Scar is going to be a bad character in the movie. Nothing appeared to tell you this. No caption came across the bottom of the screen that said "Bad Guy." No red arrow pointed to Scar and said "Evil Lion." No, you made an inference about his character based on the context clue you were given. You do the same thing when you read!

When you draw an inference or make a conclusion you are doing the same thing, you are making an educated guess based on the hints the author gives you. We call these hints "context clues." Scar trapping the innocent mouse is the context clue about Scar's character.

Usually you are making inferences and drawing conclusions the entire time that you are reading. Whether you realize it or not, you are constantly making educated guesses based on context clues. Think about a time you were reading a book and something happened that you were expecting to happen. You're not psychic! Actually, you were picking up on the context clues and making inferences about what was going to happen next!

Let's try an easy example. Read the following sentences and answer the questions at the end of the passage.

Shelly really likes to help people. She loves her job because she gets to help people every single day. However, Shelly has to work long hours and she can get called in the middle of the night for emergencies. She wears a white lab coat at work and usually she carries a stethoscope.

Pass the COOP!

What is most likely Shelly's job?

    a. Musician

    b. Lawyer

    c. Doctor

    d. Teacher

This probably seemed easy. Drawing inferences isn't always this simple, but it is the same basic principle. How did you know Shelly was a doctor? She helps people, she works long hours, she wears a white lab coat, and she gets called in for emergencies at night. Context Clues! Nowhere in the paragraph did it say Shelly was a doctor, but you were able to draw that conclusion based on the information provided in the paragraph. This is how it's done!

There is a catch, though. Remember that when you draw inferences based on reading, you should only use the information given to you by the author. Sometimes it is easy for us to make conclusions based on knowledge that is already in our mind—but that can lead you to drawing an incorrect inference. For example, let's pretend there is a bully at your school named Brent. Now let's say you read a story and the main character's name is Brent. You could NOT infer that the character in the story is a bully just because his name is Brent. You should only use the information given to you by the author to avoid drawing the wrong conclusion.

Reading and Language Arts

Let's try another example. Read the passage below, and answer the question.

Social media is an extremely popular new form of connecting and communicating over the internet. Since Facebook's original launch in 2004, millions of people have joined in the social media craze. In fact, it is estimated that almost 75% of all internet users aged 18 and older use some form of social media. Facebook started at Harvard University as a way to get students connected. However, it quickly grew into a worldwide phenomenon and today, the founder of Facebook, Mark Zuckerberg has an estimated net worth of 28.5 billion dollars.

Facebook is not the only social media platform, though. Other sites such as Twitter, Instagram, and Snapchat have since been invented and are quickly becoming just as popular! Many social media users actually use more than one type of social media. Furthermore, most social media sites have created mobile apps that allow people to connect via social media virtually anywhere in the world!

What is the most likely reason that other social media sites like Twitter and Instagram were created?

    a. Professors at Harvard University made it a class project.

    b. Facebook was extremely popular and other people thought they could also be successful by designing social media sites.

    c. Facebook was not connecting enough people.

    d. Mark Zuckerberg paid people to invent new social media sites because he wanted lots of competition.

Here, the correct answer is B. Facebook was extremely popular and other people thought they could also be successful by designing social media sites. How do we know this? What are the context clues? Take a look at the first paragraph. What do we know based on this paragraph? Well, one sentence refers to Facebook's original launch. This suggests that Facebook was one of the first social media sites. In addition, we know that the founder of Facebook has been extremely successful and is worth billions of dollars. From this we can infer that other people wanted to imitate Facebook's idea and become just as successful as Mark Zuckerberg.

Let's go through the other answers. If you chose A, it might be because Facebook started at Harvard University, so you drew the conclusion that all other social media sites were also started at Harvard University. However, there is no mention of class projects, professors, or students designing social media. So there doesn't seem to be enough support for choice A.

If you chose C, you might have been drawing your own conclusions based on outside information. Maybe none of your friends are on Facebook, so you made an inference that Facebook didn't connect enough people, so more sites were invented. Or maybe you think the people who connect on Facebook are too old, so you don't think Facebook connects enough people your age. This might be true, but remember inferences should be drawn from the information the author gives you!

If you chose D, you might be using the information that Mark Zuckerberg is worth over 28 billion dollars. It would be easy for him to pay others to design new sites, but remember, you need to use context clues! He is very wealthy, but that statement was giving you information about how successful Facebook was—not suggesting that he paid others to design more sites!

So remember, drawing inferences and conclusions is simply about using the information you are given to make an educated guess. You do this every single day so don't let this concept scare you. Look for the context clues, make sure they support your claim, and you'll be able to make accurate inferences and conclusions!

Reading and Language Arts

Meaning From Context

Often in reading comprehension questions, you are asked for the definition of a word, which you have to infer from the surrounding text, called "meaning in context." Here are a few examples with step-by-step solutions, and a few tips and tricks to answering meaning from context questions.

There are literally thousands and thousands of words in the English language. It is impossible for us to know what every single one of them means, but we also don't have time to Google a definition every time we read a word we don't understand! Even the smartest person in the world comes across words they don't know, but luckily we can use context clues to help us determine what things actually mean.

Context clues are really just little hints that can help us determine the meaning of words or phrases and honestly, the easiest way to learn how to use context clues is to practice!

Let's start with a few basic examples.

> In some countries many people are not given access to schools, teachers, or books. In these countries, people might be illiterate.

You might not know what the word illiterate means, but let's use the clues in the sentence to help us. If people are not given access to schools, teachers, or books, what might happen? They probably don't learn what we learned in school so they might not know some of the things that we learned from our teachers! Illiterate actually means "unable to read or write." This makes sense based on the context clues!

Let's work through another example.

> We have so much technology today! So much technology that many people have started using tablets and computers to read ebooks instead of

paper books! In fact, some of these people actually think that reading paper books is archaic!

Let's look for the context clues. Well, what do we know from this paragraph? We have a lot of technology and sometimes people read ebooks instead of paper books. From this we can draw the conclusion that ebooks are beginning to replace paper books because ebooks are newer and better. So if ebooks are newer and better, it must mean that paper books are older. Archaic actually means "very old or old-fashioned," which again we determined from the context clues.

Let's see if you can try a few on your own now.

> Cody noticed the strawberries in his refrigerator were old and moldy, so he abstained and threw them away.

What does abstained most likely mean?

> a. chose not to consume
> b. washed
> c. shared
> d. cut into pieces

The correct answer here is A. The context clues told you the strawberries were old and moldy and told you that Cody did something and then threw them away. If the strawberries were moldy, and Cody abstained, it makes sense that he didn't eat them—which is choice A.

You may have chosen answer B. If the strawberries were old and moldy, Cody could have washed them. But use ALL of the context clues. After he abstained, he threw them away. Why would Cody wash them and then throw them away? That doesn't make sense! In addition, why would he share them if they were old and moldy? Finally, I suppose Cody could have cut them into pieces, but why would he need to do that before throwing them away? It doesn't make as much sense, so choice A is the correct answer!

Let's do one more.

Scott had a disdain for Lily ever since she lied to their boss and got him fired.

    a. Compassion
    b. Hate
    c. Remorse
    d. Money

The correct answer is B. Scott was fired because Lily lied. Can you imagine if this happened to you? I think you would have some pretty strong feelings just like Scott!

It's simple! By understanding the context, you can determine the meaning of even the hardest of words!

English Grammar Self-Assessment

```
   A B C D
 1 ○ ○ ○ ○
 2 ○ ○ ○ ○
 3 ○ ○ ○ ○
 4 ○ ○ ○ ○
 5 ○ ○ ○ ○
 6 ○ ○ ○ ○
 7 ○ ○ ○ ○
 8 ○ ○ ○ ○
 9 ○ ○ ○ ○
10 ○ ○ ○ ○
11 ○ ○ ○ ○
12 ○ ○ ○ ○
13 ○ ○ ○ ○
14 ○ ○ ○ ○
15 ○ ○ ○ ○
16 ○ ○ ○ ○
17 ○ ○ ○ ○
18 ○ ○ ○ ○
19 ○ ○ ○ ○
20 ○ ○ ○ ○
```

Reading and Language Arts

English Grammar Self-Assessment

Choose the phrase which best completes the sentence.

1. The Ford Motor Company was named for Henry Ford, _____.

    a. which had founded the company.

    b. who founded the company.

    c. whose had founded the company.

    d. whom had founded the company.

2. Thomas Edison _____ since he invented the light bulb, television, motion pictures, and phonograph.

    a. has always been known as the greatest inventor

    b. was always been known as the greatest inventor

    c. must have had been always known as the greatest inventor

    d. will had been known as the greatest inventor

3. The weatherman on Channel 6 said that this has been the _____.

    a. most hotter summer on record

    b. most hottest summer on record

    c. hottest summer on record

    d. hotter summer on record

4. **Although Joe is tall for his age, his brother Elliot is _____ of the two.**

   a. the tallest

   b. more tallest

   c. the tall

   d. the taller

5. **When KISS came to town, all of the tickets _____ before I could buy one.**

   a. will be sold out

   b. had been sold out

   c. were being sold out

   d. was sold out

6. **Choose the sentence with the correct grammar.**

   a. He would have postponed the camping trip, if he would have known about the forecast.

   b. If he would have known about the forecast, he would have postponed the camping trip.

   c. If he have known about the forecast, he would have postponed the camping trip.

   d. If he had known about the forecast, he would have postponed the camping trip.

Reading and Language Arts

7. Choose the sentence with the correct grammar.

a. If Joe had told me the truth, I wouldn't have been so angry.

b. If Joe would have told me the truth, I wouldn't have been so angry.

c. I wouldn't have been so angry if Joe would have told the truth.

d. If Joe would have telled me the truth, I wouldn't have been so angry.

8. Choose the sentence with the correct grammar.

a. He doesn't have any money to buy clothes, and neither do I.

b. He doesn't have any money to buy clothes, and neither does I.

c. He don't have any money to buy clothes, and neither do I.

d. He don't have any money to buy clothes, and neither does I.

9. Choose the sentence with the correct grammar.

a. Because it really don't matter, I don't care if I go there.

b. Because it really doesn't matter, I doesn't care if I go there.

c. Because it really doesn't matter, I don't care if I go there.

d. Because it really don't matter, I don't care if I go there.

10. Choose the sentence with the correct grammar.

a. The dog took the stuffed toy to his master's empty chair.

b. The dog brang the stuffed toy to his master's empty chair.

c. The dog brought the stuffed toy to his master's empty chair.

d. The dog taken the stuffed toy to his master's empty chair.

Select the Best Revision.

11. When I was a child, my mother taught me to say thank you, holding the door open for other, and cover my mouth when yawning or coughing.

a. When I was a child, my mother teaching me to say thank you, to hold the door open for others, and cover my mouth when yawning or coughing.

b. When I was a child, my mother taught me say thank you, to hold the door open for others, and to covering my mouth when yawning or coughing.

c. When I was a child, my mother taught me saying thank you, holding the door open for others, and to cover my mouth when yawning or coughing.

d. When I was a child, my mother taught me to say thank you, hold the door open for others, and cover my mouth when yawning or coughing.

Reading and Language Arts

12. Mother is talking to a man that wants to hire her to be a receptionist.

    a. Mother is talking to a man who wants to hire her to be a receptionist.

    b. Mother is talked to a man who wants to hire her to be a receptionist.

    c. Mother is talking to a man who wants to her. To be a receptionist.

    d. Mother is talking to a man hiring her who to be a receptionist.

Select The Correct Word Or Phrase For The Blank.

13. All of the people at the school, including the teachers and _____ were glad when summer break came.

    a. students:

    b. students,

    c. students;

    d. students

14. To _____, Anne was on time for her math class.

    a. everybody's surprise

    b. every body's surprise

    c. everybodys surprise

    d. everybodys' surprise

15. If he _____ the textbook like he was supposed to, he would have known what was on the test.

    a. will have read

    b. shouldn't have read

    c. would have read

    d. had read

16. Following the tornado, telephone poles _____ all over the street.

    a. laid

    b. lied

    c. were lying

    d. were laying

Select the correct version of the sentences below.

17. Politics <u>are</u> his chief interest.

    a. Politics is his chief interest.

    b. Politics are his chief interests.

    c. Politics is his chief interests.

    d. The sentence is correct.

18. He is a <u>cowered</u> person.

    a. He is a cowardest person.

    b. He is a cowardly person.

    c. He is a coward person.

    d. The sentence is correct.

Reading and Language Arts

19. Why did Mr. Simpson <u>deny</u> to help you?

    a. Why did Mr. Simpson refuse to help you?

    b. Why did Mr. Simpson resist to help you?

    c. Why did Mr. Simpson not accept to help you?

    d. The sentence is correct.

20. She is the <u>most cleverest</u> girl in the class.

    a. She is the most clever girl in the class.

    b. She is the cleverest girl in the class.

    c. She is the most cleverer girl in the class.

    d. The sentence is correct.

Part II – Language Arts Answer Key

1. B
The sentence refers to a person, so "who" is the only correct option.

2. A
The sentence requires the past perfect "has always been known." Furthermore, this is the only grammatically correct choice.

3. C
The superlative, "hottest," is used when expressing a temperature greater than that of anything to which it is being compared.

4. D
When comparing two items, use "the taller." When comparing more than two items, use "the tallest."

5. B
The past perfect form is used to describe an event that occurred in the past, and prior to another event.

6. D
The third conditional is used for talking about an unreal situation (a situation that did not happen) in the past. For example, "If I had studied harder, [if clause] I would have passed the exam [main clause]. This has the same meaning as, "I failed the exam because I didn't study hard enough."

7. A
The third conditional is used for talking about an unreal situation (a situation that did not happen) in the past. For example, "If I had studied harder, [if clause] I would have passed the exam [main clause]. This has the same meaning as, "I failed the exam because I didn't study hard enough."

8. A
Shows agreement with a negative statement by using "neither."

Reading and Language Arts

9. C
Doesn't, does not, or does is used with the third person singular--the pronouns he, she, and it. Don't, do not, or do is used with first, second, and third person plural.

10. A
Whether to use "bring" or "take" depends on location. Something coming toward the subject's location is brought. Something going away from the subject's location is taken.

11. D
The sentence starts with a phrase, which is separated by a comma and then lists the things the speaker's mother taught, to say thank you, etc. Each item is separated by a comma.

12. A
When referring to a person, use "who" instead of "that."

13. B
The comma separates a phrase.

14. A
Possessive pronouns ending in s take an apostrophe before the 's': one's; everyone's; somebody's, nobody else's, etc.

15. D
When talking about something that didn't happen in the past, use the past perfect (if I had done).

16. C
"Lie" means to recline, and does not take an object. "Lay" means to place and does take an object. Peter lay the books on the table (the books are the direct object), or the telephone poles were lying on the road (no direct object).

17. A
Despite 's' ending, "politics" is a singular noun.

18. B
"Cowardly" is an adjective used to modify a person.

19. A
"Deny" means to reject or disagree with the truth of something. "Refuse" means to decline to do or accept something.

20. B
"Cleverest" is the superlative form, and means the most clever.

How to Answer English Grammar Multiple Choice - Verb Tense

This tutorial is designed to help you answer English Grammar multiple choice questions as well as a very quick refresher on verb tenses. It is assumed that you have some familiarity with the verb tenses covered here. If you find these questions difficulty or do not understand the tense construction, we recommend you seek out additional instruction.

Tenses Covered

1. Past Progressive
2. Present Perfect
3. Present Perfect Progressive
4. Present Progressive
5. Simple Future
6. Simple Future – "Going to" Form
7. Past Perfect Progressive
8. Future Perfect Progressive
9. Future Perfect
10. Future Progressive
11. Past Perfect

1. The Past Progressive Tense

How to Recognize This Tense

He *was running* very fast when he fell.

They *were drinking* coffee when he arrived.

About the Past Progressive Tense

This tense is used to speak of an action that was in progress in the past when another event occurred.

The action was unfolding at a point in the past.

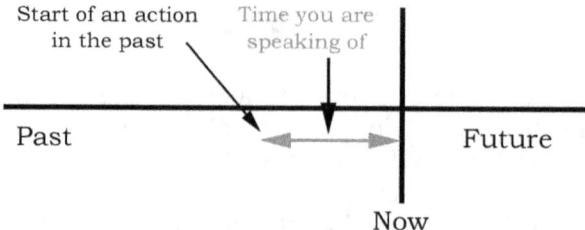

Past Progressive Tense Construction

This tense is formed by using the past tense of the verb "to be" plus the present participle of the main verb.

Sample Question

Bill _____ lunch when we arrived.

   a. will eat
   b. is eating
   c. eats
   d. was eating

How to Answer This Type of Question

1. First examine the question for clues about the time frame.

The sentence ends with "when we arrived," so we know the time frame is a point ("when") in the past (arrived).

The correct answer will refer to an ongoing action at a point of time in the past.

Reading and Language Arts

2. Examine the choices and eliminate any obviously incorrect answers.

Choice A is the future tense so we can eliminate.

Choice B is the present continuous so we can eliminate.

Choice C is present tense so we can eliminate.

Choice D refers to an action that takes place at a point of time in the past ("was eating").

2. The Present Perfect Tense

How to Recognize This Tense

I *have had* enough to eat.

We *have been* to Paris many times.

I *have known* him for five years.

I *have been* coming here since I was a child.

About the Present Perfect Tense

This tense expresses the idea that something happened (or didn't happen) at an unspecific time in the past up until the present. The action happened at an unspecified time in the past. (If there is a specific time mentioned, the simple past tense is used.) It can be used for repeated action, accomplishments, changes over time and uncompleted action.

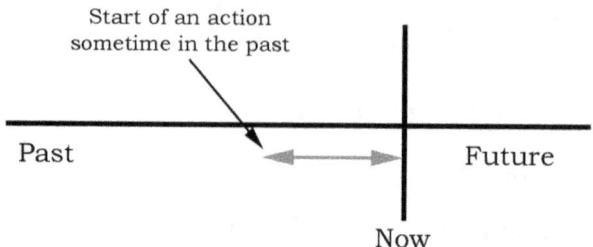

Present Perfect Tense Construction

It is also used with "for" and "since."

This tense is formed by using the present tense of the verb "to have" plus the past participle of the main verb.

Sample Question

I _____ these birds many times.

    a. am seeing
    b. will saw
    c. have seen
    d. have saw

How to Answer This Type of Question

1. First examine the question for clues about the time frame.

"Many times" tells us that the action is repeated and in the past.

2. Examine the choices and eliminate any obviously incorrect answers.

Choice A, "am seeing" is incorrect because it is a continuing action, i.e. in the present; it also doesn't use a form of 'have'.

Reading and Language Arts

Choice B is grammatically incorrect.

Choice C is tells of something that has happened in the past and is now over. Best choice so far.

Choice D is grammatically incorrect.

3. The Present Perfect Progressive Tense

How to Recognize This Tense

We *have been seeing* a lot of rainy days.

I *have been reading* some very good books.

About the Present Perfect Progressive Tense

This tense expresses the idea that something happened (or didn't happen) in the relatively recent past, but <u>the action is not finished.</u> It is used to express the duration of the action.

NOTE: The present perfect speaks of an action that happened sometime in the past, but this action is finished. In the present perfect progressive tense, the action that started in the past is still going on.

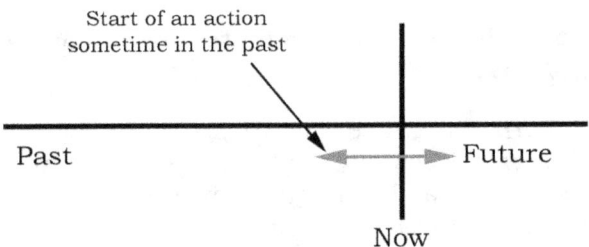

Present Perfect Progressive Tense Construction

This tense is formed by using the present tense of the verb "to have," plus "been," plus the present participle of the main verb.

Sample Question

Bill _____ there for two hours.

    a. sits

    b. sitting

    c. has been sitting

    d. will sat

How to Answer This Type of Question

1. First examine the question for clues about the time frame.

"For two hours" tells us that the action, "sits," is continuous up to now, and may continue into the future.

Note this sentence could also be the simple past tense,

Bill sat there for two hours.

Or the future tense,

Bill will sit there for two hours.

However, these are not among the options.

2. Examine the choices and eliminate any obviously incorrect answers.

Choice A is incorrect because it is the present tense.
Choice B is incorrect because it is the present continuous.
Choice C is correct. "Has been sitting" expresses a continuous action in the past that isn't finished.
Choice D is grammatically incorrect.

4. The Present Progressive Tense

How to Recognize This Tense

We *are having* a delicious lunch.

They *are driving* much too fast.

About the Present Progressive Tense

This tense is used to express what the action is <u>right now</u>. The action started in the recent past, and is continuing into the future.

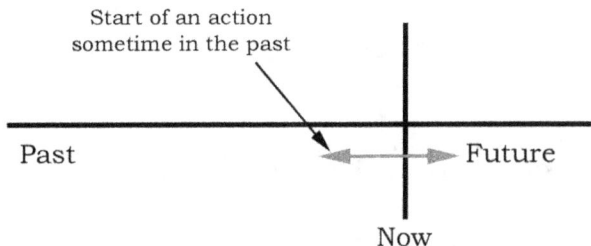

Present Perfect Tense Construction

The Present Progressive Tense is formed by using the present tense of "to be" plus the present participle of the main verb.

Sample Question

She _____ very hard these days.

    a. works

    b. is working

    c. will work

    d. worked

How to Answer This Type of Question

1. First examine the question for clues about the time frame.

The end of the sentence includes "these days" which tell us the action started in the past, continues into the present, and may continue into the future.

2. Examine the choices and eliminate any obviously incorrect answers.

Choice A, the simple present is incorrect.
Choice B, "is working" is correct.
Check the other two choices just to be sure. Choice C is future tense, and Choice D is past tense, so they can be eliminated.

The correct answer is Choice B.

5. The Simple Future Tense

How to Recognize This Tense

I *will see* you tomorrow.
We *will drive* the car.

About the Simple Future Tense

This tense shows that the action will happen some time in the future.

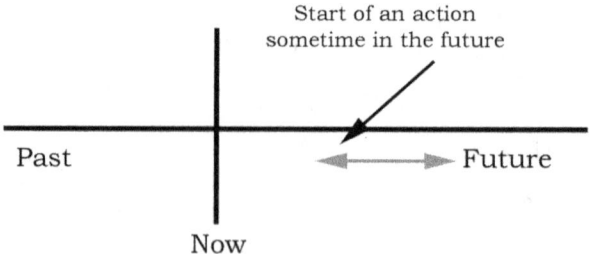

Simple Future Tense Construction

The tense is formed by using "will" plus the root form of the verb. (The root form of the verb is the infinitive without "to." Examples: read, swim.)

Sample Question

We _____ to Paris next year.

    a. went

    b. had been

    c. will go

    d. go

How to Answer This Type of Question

1. First examine the question for clues about the time frame.

The last two words of the sentence, "next year," clearly identify this sentence as referring to the future.

2. Examine the choices and eliminate any obviously incorrect answers.

Choice A is the past tense and can be eliminated.

Choice B is the past perfect tense and can be eliminated.

Choice D is the simple present and can be eliminated.

Choice C is the only one left and is the correct simple future tense.

6. The Simple Future Tense – The "Going to" Form

How to Recognize This Tense

I *am going to* see you tomorrow.

We *are going to* drive the car.

About the Simple Future Tense

This form of the future tense is used to show the intention of doing something in the future. (This is the strict grammatical meaning, but in daily speech, it is often used interchangeably with the simple future tense, the "will" form.)

The tense is formed by using the present conditional tense of "to go," plus the infinitive of the verb.

Sample Question

I _____ shopping in an hour.

    a. go

    b. have gone

    c. am going to go

    d. went

How to Answer This Type of Question

1. First examine the question for clues about the time frame.

"In an hour" clearly identifies the action as taking place in the future.

2. Examine the choices and eliminate any obviously incorrect answers.

Choice A is the simple present tense and can be eliminated.

Choice B is the past perfect and can be eliminated.

Choice C is the correct answer.

Choice D is the past tense and can be eliminated.

7. The Past Perfect Progressive Tense

How to Recognize This Tense

I *had been sleeping* for an hour when you phoned.

We *had been eating* our dinner when they all came into the dining room.

About the Past Perfect Progressive Tense

This tense is used to show that the action had been going on for a period of time in the past when another action, also in the past, occurred.

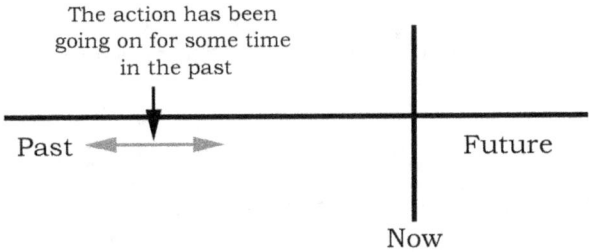

Past Perfect Tense Construction

The tense is formed by using the past perfect tense of the verb "to be" plus the present participle of the main verb.

Sample Question

How long _____ you _____ when I saw you?

      a. are _____ running

      b. had _____ running

      c. had _____ been running

      d. was _____ running

How to Answer This Type of Question

1. First examine the question for clues about the time frame.

"When I saw" tells us the sentence happened at a point of time ("when") in the past ("saw").

2. Examine the choices and eliminate any obviously incorrect answers.

Choice A, "are running" is incorrect and can be eliminated.

Choice B, "Had ___ running" is grammatically incorrect and can be eliminated.

Choice C is correct.

Choice D is grammatically incorrect so the answer is Choice C.

8. Future Perfect Progressive Tense

How to Recognize This Tense

I *will have been working* here for two years in March.

I *will have been driving* for four hours when I get there, so I will be tired.

About the Future Perfect Progressive Tense

This tense is used to show that the action continues up to a point of time in the future.

Future Prefect Progressive Tense Construction

This tense is formed by using the future perfect tense of "to be" plus the present participle of the main verb.

Reading and Language Arts

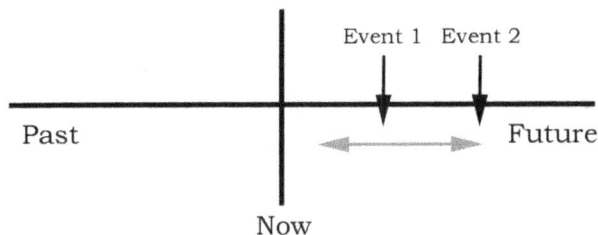

Sample Question

_____ you _____ all the time I am gone?

    a. have _____ been working

    b. will _____ have been working

    c. are _____ worked

    d. will _____ worked

How to Answer This Type of Question

1. First examine the question for clues about the time frame.

"All the time I am gone" refers to an action in the future ("time I am gone") and the action is progressive ("all the time"). The progressive action means the correct choice will be a verb tense that ends in "ing."

2. Examine the choices and eliminate any obviously incorrect answers.

Choice A, the past perfect, refers to a past continuous event and is also grammatically incorrect in the sentence, so Choice A can be eliminated.

Choice B looks correct because it refers to an action will be going on for a period of time in the future.

Examine Choices C and D just to be sure. Both choices are grammatically incorrect and can be eliminated.

Choice B is the correct answer.

9. The Future Perfect Tense

How to Recognize This Tense

By next November, I *will have received* my promotion.

By the time he gets home, she is going *to have cleaned* the entire house.

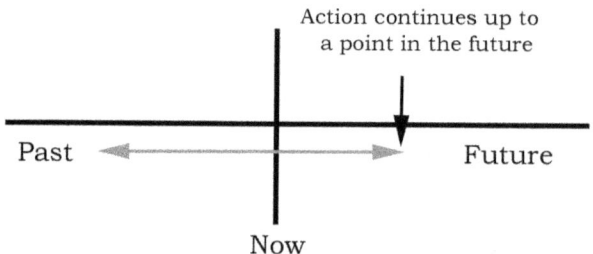

About the Future Perfect Tense

The future perfect tense expresses action in the future before another action in the future. This is the past in the future. For example:

He *will have prepared* dinner when she arrives.

Future Perfect Tense Construction

This tense is formed by "will + have + past participle."

Reading and Language Arts

Sample Question

They _____ their seats before the game begins.

    a. will have find
    b. will find
    c. will have found
    d. found

How to Answer This Type of Question

1. First examine the question for clues about the time frame.

This question could be several different tenses. The only clue about the time frame is "before the game begins," which refers to a specific point of time.

We know it isn't in the past, because "begins" is incorrect for the past tense. Similarly with the present. So the question is about something that happens in the future, before another event in the future.

2. Examine the choices and eliminate any obviously incorrect answers.

Choice A can be eliminated as incorrect.
Choice B looks good, so mark it and check the others before making a final decision.
Choice C is the past perfect and can be eliminated because the time frame is incorrect.
Choice D is the simple past tense and can be eliminated for the same reason.

10. Future Progressive Tense

How to Recognize This Tense

The teams *will be playing* soccer when we arrive.

At 3:45 the soccer fans *will be waiting* for the game to start at 4:00 o'clock

At 3:45 the soccer players *will be preparing* to play at 4:00 o'clock

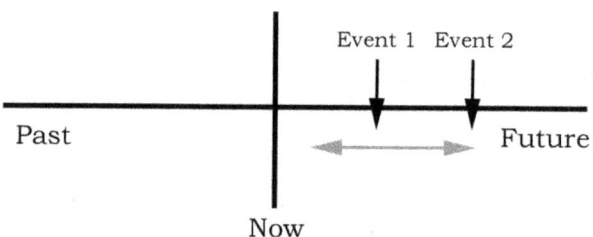

About the Future Progressive Tense

The future progressive tense talks about a continuing action in the future.

Future Progressive Tense Construction

will+ be + (root form) + ing = will be playing

Sample Question

Many excited fans _____ a bus to see the game at 4:00.

    a. catch

    b. catching

    c. have been catching

    d. will be catching

Reading and Language Arts

How to Answer This Type of Question

1. First examine the question for clues about the time frame.

"At 4:00," tells us the sentence is either in the past OR in the future.

2. Examine the choices and eliminate any obviously incorrect answers.

From the time frame of the sentence, the answer will be past or future tense.

Choice A is the present tense and can be eliminated.
Choice B is the present continuous tense and can be eliminated.
Choice C is the past perfect continuous and can be eliminated.
Choice D is the only one left. Quickly examining the tense, it is future progressive and is correct in the sentence.

11. The Past Perfect Tense

How to Recognize This Tense

The party *had* just *started* when the coach arrived.

We *had waited* for twenty minutes when the bus finally came.

About the Past Perfect

The past perfect tense talks about two events that happened in the past and establishes which event happened first.

Another example is, "We had eaten when he arrived."

The two events are "eat" and "he arrived." From the sentence above the past perfect tense tells us the first event, "eat" happened before the second event, "he arrived."

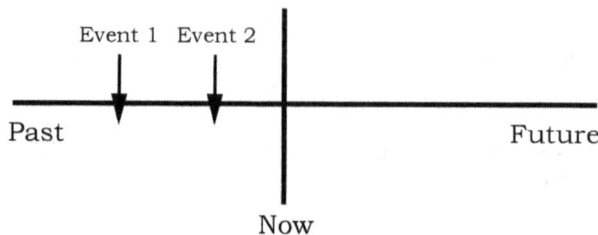

I had already eaten when my friends arrived.

Past Perfect Tense Construction

The past perfect is formed by "have" plus the past participle.

Sample Question

It was time to go home after they _____ the game.

    a. will win

    b. win

    c. had won

    d. wins

How to Answer This Type of Question

1. First examine the question for clues about the time frame.

"Was" tells us the sentence happened in the past. Also notice there are two events, "go home" and "after the game."

2. Examine the choices and eliminate any obviously incorrect answers.

Choice A is the future tense and can be eliminated. Choice B is the simple present and can be eliminated. Choice C is the past perfect and orders the two events in the past.

Choice D is the present tense and incorrect and can be eliminated, so Choice C is the correct answer.

Common English Usage Mistakes - A Quick Review

Like some parts of English grammar, usage is definitely going to be on the exam and there isn't any tricky strategies or Short-cuts to help you get through this section.
Here is a quick review of common usage mistakes.

1. May and Might

'May' can act as a principal verb, which can express permission or possibility.

Examples:

Lets wait, the meeting may have started.
May I begin now?

'May' can act as an auxiliary verb, which an expresses a purpose or wish

Examples:

May you find favour in the sight of your employer.

May your wishes come true.
People go to school so that they may be educated.

The past tense of may is might.

Examples:

I asked if I might begin

'Might' can be used to signify a weak or slim possibility or polite suggestion.

Examples:

You might find him in his office, but I doubt it.
You might offer to help if you want to.

2. Lie and Lay

The verb lay should always take an object. The three forms of the verb lay are: laid, lay and laid.

The verb lie (recline) should not take any object. The three forms of the verb lie are: lay, lie and lain.

Examples:

Lay on the bed.
The tables were laid by the students.
Let the little kid lie.
The patient lay on the table.

The dog has lain there for 30 minutes.

Note: The verb lie can also mean "to tell a falsehood." This verb can appear in three forms: lied, lie, and lied. This is different from the verb lie (recline) mentioned above.

Examples:

The accused is fond of telling lies.
Did she lie?

3. Would and should

The past tense of shall is 'should', and so "should" generally follows the same principles as "shall."

The past tense of will is "would," and so "would" generally

follows the same principles as "will."

The two verbs 'would and should' can be correctly used interchangeably to signify obligation. The two verbs also have some unique uses too. Should is used in three persons to signify obligation.

Examples:

I should go after work.
People should exercise everyday.
You should be generous.

"Would" is specially used in any of the three persons, to signify willingness, determination and habitual action.

Examples:

They would go for a test run every Saturday.
They would not ignore their duties.
She would try to be punctual.

4. Principle and Auxiliary Verbs

Two principal verbs can be used along with one auxiliary verb as long as the auxiliary verb form suits the two principal verbs.

Examples:

Several people have been employed and some promoted.

A new tree has been planted and the old has been cut down.

Again note the difference in the verb form.

5. Can and Could

A. Can is used to express capacity or ability.
Examples:

I can complete the assignment today
He can meet his target.

B. Can is also used to express permission.

Examples:

Yes, you can begin

In the sentence below, "can" was used to mean the same thing as "may." However, the difference is that the word "can" is used for negative or interrogative sentences, while "may" is used in affirmative sentences to express possibility.

Examples:

They may be correct.   Positive sentence - use may.
Can this statement be correct? A question using "can."
It cannot be correct. Negative sentence using "can."

The past tense of can is could. It can serve as a principal verb when it is used to express its own meaning.

Examples:

Despite the difficulty of the test, he could still perform well. "Could" here is used to express ability.

6. Ought

The verb ought should normally be followed by the word to.

Reading and Language Arts

Examples:

I *ought to* close shop now.

The verb 'ought' expresses:

A. Desirability

You ought to wash your hands before eating. It is desirable to wash your hands.

B. Probability

She ought to be on her way back by now. She is probably on her way.

C. Moral obligation or duty

The government ought to protect the oppressed. It is the government's duty to protect the oppressed.

7. Raise and Rise

Rise
The verb rise means to go up, or to ascend.
The verb rise can appear in three forms, rose, rise, and risen. The verb should not take an object.

Examples:

The bird rose very slowly.
The trees rise above the house.
My aunt has risen in her career.

Raise
The verb raise means to increase, to lift up.
The verb raise can appear in three forms, raised, raise and raised.

Examples:

He raised his hand.
The workers requested a raise.
Do not raise that subject.

8. Past Tense and Past Participle

Pay attention to the proper use of these verbs: sing, show, ring, awake, fly, flow, begin, hang and sink.

Mistakes usually occur when using the past participle and past tense of these verbs as they are often mixed up.

Each of these verbs can appear in three forms:

Sing, Sang, Sung.
Show, Showed, Showed/Shown.
Ring, Rang, Rung.
Awake, awoke, awaken
Fly, Flew, Flown.
Flow, Flowed, Flowed.
Begin, Began, Begun.
Hang, Hanged, Hanged (a criminal)
Hang, Hung, Hung (a picture)
Sink, Sank, Sunk.

Examples:

The stranger rang the door bell. (simple past tense)
I have rung the door bell already. (past participle - an action completed in the past)

The stone sank in the river. (simple past tense)
The stone had already sunk. (past participle - an action completed in the past)

The meeting began at 4:00.
The meeting has begun.

9. Shall and Will

When speaking informally, the two can be used interchangeably. In formal writing, they must be used correctly.

"Will" is used in the second or third person, while "shall" is used in the first person. Both verbs are used to express a time or even in the future.

Examples:

I shall, We shall (First Person)
You will (Second Person)
They will (Third Person)

This principle however reverses when the verbs are to be used to express threats, determination, command, willingness, promise or compulsion. In these instances, will is now used in first person and shall in the second and third person.

Examples:

I will be there next week, no matter what.
This is a promise, so the first person "I" takes "will."

You shall ensure that the work is completed.
This is a command, so the second person "you" takes "shall."

I will try to make payments as promised.
This is a promise, so the first person "I" takes "will."

They shall have arrived by the end of the day.
This is a determination, so the third person "they" takes shall.

Note
A. The two verbs, shall and will should not occur twice in the same sentence when the same future is being referred to

Example:

I shall arrive early if my driver is here on time.

B. Will should not be used in the first person when questions are being asked
Examples:

Shall I go ?
Shall we go?

Subject Verb Agreement

Verbs in any sentence must agree with the subject of the sentence in person and number. Problems usually occur when the verb doesn't correspond with the right subject or the verb fails to match the noun close to it.

Unfortunately, there is no easy way around these principals - no tricky strategy or easy rule. You just have to memorize them.

Here is a quick review:

The verb to be, present (past)

Person	Singular	Plural
First	I am (was)	we are (were)
Second	you are (were)	you are (were)
Third	he, she, it is (was)	they are (were)

The verb to have, present (past)

Person	Singular	Plural
First	I have (had)	we have (had)
Second	you have (had)	you have (had)
Third	he, she, it has (had)	they have (had)

Regular verbs, e.g. to walk, present (past)

Person	Singular	Plural
First	I walk (walked)	we walk (walked)
Second	you walk (walked)	you walk (walked)
Third	he, she, it walks (walked)	they work (walked)

1. Every and Each

When nouns are qualified by "every" or "each," they take a singular verb even if they are joined by 'and'

Examples:

Each mother and daughter *was* a given separate test.
Every teacher and student *was* properly welcomed.

2. Plural Nouns

Nouns like measles, tongs, trousers, riches, scissors etc. are all plural.

Examples:

The trousers *are* dirty.
My scissors *have* gone missing.
The tongs *are* on the table.

3. With and As Well

Two subjects linked with "with" or "as well" should have a verb that matches the first subject.

Examples:

The pencil, with the papers and equipment, *is* on the desk.
David as well as Louis is coming.

4. Plural Nouns

The following nouns take a singular verb:

> politics, mathematics, innings, news, advice, summons, furniture, information, poetry, machinery, vacation, scenery

Examples:

The machinery *is* difficult to assemble
The furniture *has* been delivered
The scenery *was* beautiful

5. Single Entities

A proper noun in plural form that refers to a single entity requires a singular verb. This is a complicated way of saying; some things appear to be plural, but are really singular, or some nouns refer to a collection of things but the collection is really singular.

Examples:

The United Nations Organization *is* the decision maker in the matter.

Here the "United Nations Organization" is really only one "thing" or noun, but is made up of many "nations."

The book, "The Seven Virgins" *was* not available in the library.

Here there is only one book, although the title of the book is plural.

6. Specific Amounts are always singular

A plural noun that refers to a specific amount or quantity that is considered as a whole (dozen, hundred, score etc) requires a singular verb.

Examples:

60 minutes *is* quite a long time.
Here "60 minutes" is considered a whole, and therefore one item (singular noun).

The first million is the most difficult.

7. Either, Neither and Each are always singular

The verb is always singular when used with: either, each, neither, every one and many.

Examples:

Either of the boys *is* lying.
Each of the employees *has* been well compensated
Many a police officer *has* been found to be courageous
Every one of the teachers *is* responsible

8. Linking with Either, Or, and Neither match the second subject

Two subjects linked by "either," "or,""nor" or "neither" should have a verb that matches the second subject.

Examples:

Neither David nor Paul *will* be coming.
Either Mary or Tina *is* paying.

Note
If one of the subjects linked by "either," "or,""nor" or "neither" is in plural form, then the verb should also be in plural, and the verb should be close to the plural subject.
Examples:
Neither the mother *nor* her kids *have* eaten.
Either Mary *or* her *friends are* paying.

9. Collective Nouns are Plural

Some collective nouns such as poultry, gentry, cattle, vermin etc. are considered plural and require a plural verb.

Examples:

The *poultry are* sick.
The *cattle are* well fed.

Note
Collective nouns involving people can work with both plural and singular verbs.

Examples:

Nigerians are known to be hard working
Europeans live in Africa

10. Nouns that are Singular and Plural

Nouns like deer, sheep, swine, salmon etc. can be singular or plural and require the same verb form.

Examples:

The swine is feeding. (singular)
The swine are feeding. (plural)

The salmon is on the table. (singular)
The salmon are running upstream. (plural)

11. Collective Nouns are Singular

Collective nouns such as Army, Jury, Assembly, Committee, Team etc should carry a singular verb when they subscribe to one idea. If the ideas or views are more than one, then the verb used should be plural.

Examples:

The committee is in agreement in their decision.

The committee were in disagreement in their decision.
The jury has agreed on a verdict.
The jury were unable to agree on a verdict.

12. Subjects links by "and" are plural.

Two subjects linked by "and" always require a plural verb

Examples:

David and John are students.

Note
If the subjects linked by "and" are used as one phrase, or constitute one idea, then the verb must be singular

The color of his socks and shoe is black.
Here "socks and shoe" are two nouns, however the subject is "color" which is singular.

MATHEMATICS

THIS SECTION CONTAINS A MATH SELF-ASSESSMENT MATH TUTORIALS. The Tutorials are designed to familiarize general principles and the Self-Assessment contains general questions similar to the math questions likely to be on the COOP exam, but are not intended to be identical to the exam questions. The tutorials are not designed to be a complete math course, and it is assumed that students have some familiarity with math. If you do not understand parts of the tutorial, or find the tutorial difficult, it is recommended that you seek out additional instruction.

Mathematics Self-assessment

Below is a Mathematics Self-assessment. The purpose of the self-assessment is:

- Identify your strengths and weaknesses.
- Develop your personalized study plan (above)
- Get accustomed to the COOP format
- Extra practice – the self-assessments are almost a full 3rd practice test!

Since this is a Self-assessment, and depending on how confident you are with Math, timing yourself is optional.

The COOP includes a comprehensive Math Exam that covers decimals, whole numbers, fractions, number system conversions, percent, and basic geometry. There are a total of 40 questions, which must be answered in 35 minutes. The self-assessment has 40 questions, so allow 35 minutes to complete this assessment.

The questions below are not the same as you will find on the COOP - that would be too easy! And nobody knows

Mathematics

what the questions will be and they change all the time. Below are general Math questions that cover the same areas as the COOP. So, while the format and exact wording of the questions may differ slightly, and change from year to year, if you can answer the questions below, you will have no problem with the Math section of the COOP.

The self-assessment is designed to give you a baseline score in the different areas covered. Here is a brief outline of how your score on the self-assessment relates to your understanding of the material.

75% - 100%	Excellent – you have mastered the content
50 – 75%	Good. You have a working knowledge. Even though you can just pass this section, you may want to review the tutorials and do some extra practice to see if you can improve your mark.
25% - 50%	Below Average. You do not understand the content. Review the tutorials, and retake this quiz again in a few days, before proceeding to the rest of the study guide.
Less than 25%	Poor. You have a very limited understanding. Please review the Tutorials, and retake this quiz again in a few days, before proceeding to the rest of the study guide.

Math Self-Assessment

	A	B	C	D	E		A	B	C	D	E
1	○	○	○	○	○	26	○	○	○	○	○
2	○	○	○	○	○	27	○	○	○	○	○
3	○	○	○	○	○	28	○	○	○	○	○
4	○	○	○	○	○	29	○	○	○	○	○
5	○	○	○	○	○	30	○	○	○	○	○
6	○	○	○	○	○	31	○	○	○	○	○
7	○	○	○	○	○	32	○	○	○	○	○
8	○	○	○	○	○	33	○	○	○	○	○
9	○	○	○	○	○	34	○	○	○	○	○
10	○	○	○	○	○	35	○	○	○	○	○
11	○	○	○	○	○	36	○	○	○	○	○
12	○	○	○	○	○	37	○	○	○	○	○
13	○	○	○	○	○	38	○	○	○	○	○
14	○	○	○	○	○	39	○	○	○	○	○
15	○	○	○	○	○	40	○	○	○	○	○
16	○	○	○	○	○	41	○	○	○	○	○
17	○	○	○	○	○	42	○	○	○	○	○
18	○	○	○	○	○	43	○	○	○	○	○
19	○	○	○	○	○	44	○	○	○	○	○
20	○	○	○	○	○	45	○	○	○	○	○
21	○	○	○	○	○						
22	○	○	○	○	○						
23	○	○	○	○	○						
24	○	○	○	○	○						
25	○	○	○	○	○						

Math Self-Assessment

1. A boy has 5 red balls, 3 white balls and 2 yellow balls. What percent of the balls are yellow?

    a. 2%
    b. 8%
    c. 20%
    d. 12%

2. The length a rectangle is twice its width and its area is equal to the area of a square of side 12 cm. What will be the perimeter of the rectangle near to the nearest whole number?

    a. 36 cm
    b. 46 cm
    c. 51 cm
    d. 56 cm

3. There are 15 yellow and 35 orange balls in a basket. How many more yellow balls must be added to make yellow balls 65%?

    a. 35
    b. 50
    c. 65
    d. 70

4. At the beginning of 2009, Marilyn invested $5,000 in a savings account. The account pays 4% interest per year. At the end of the year, after the interest was paid, how much did Marilyn have in the account?

    a. $5,200
    b. $5,020
    c. $5,110
    d. $7,000

5. The average weight of 13 students in a class of 15 (two were absent that day) is 42 kg. When the remaining 2 were weighed, the average became 42.7 kg. If one of the remaining students weighs 48, how much does the other weigh?

    a. 44.7 kg.

    b. 45.6 kg.

    c. 46.5 kg.

    d. 47.4 kg.

6. The total expense of building a fence around a square field is $2000 at a rate of $5 per meter. What is the length of one side?

    a. 40 meters

    b. 80 meters

    c. 100 meters

    d. 320 meters

7. Convert 23.67 to percent.

    a. 2.367%

    b 236.7%

    c. 23.67%

    d. 2367%

8. If 144 students need to go on a trip and the buses carry 36 students each, how many buses do they need?

    a. 6

    b. 5

    c. 4

    d. 3

Mathematics

9. A mother is making spaghetti for her son. The recipe calls for 500 grams of spaghetti, and 0.75 grams of salt. However, the mom just wants 125 grams of spaghetti. How much salt should she use?

   a. 0.38 grams
   b. 0.75 grams
   c. 0.19 grams
   d. 0.25 grams

10. A young student deposits $200 in a savings account hoping to buy a bicycle worth $245. If the bank offers a 15% interest rate, how long will the boy have to wait?

   a. 1½ years
   b. 2 ½ years
   c. 2 years
   d. 1 year

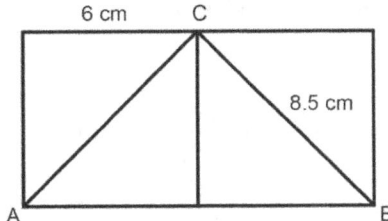

Note: figure not drawn to scale

11. Assuming the quadrangles are identical rectangles, what is the perimeter of △ABC in the above shape?

   a. 25.5 cm
   b. 27 cm
   c. 30 cm
   d. 29 cm

12. A pet store had total sales of $19,304.56 for the month of June. If the wholesale cost was $5,284.34, the employees were paid $8,384.76, and the rent was $2,920.00, how much profit did the store make in June?

    a. $5,635.46
    b. $2,714.47
    c. $14,020.22
    d. $10,019.80

13. Tony bought 15 dozen eggs for $80. 16 eggs were broken during loading and unloading. He sold the remainder for $0.54 each. What will be his percent profit? Provide answer in 2 significant digits.

    a. 11%
    b. 11.2%
    c. 11.5%
    d. 12%

14. The sale price of a car is $12,590, which is 20% off the original price. What is the original price?

    a. $14,310.40
    b. $14,990.90
    c. $15,108.00
    d. $15,737.50

15. Estimate 16 x 230.

    a. 31,000
    b. 301,000
    c. 3,100
    d. 3,000,000

Mathematics

16. In a small village there are 9 families with 3 children, 8 families with 2 children, and 4 families having 5 children. What is the average number of children in a family?

    a. 2.5
    b. 2.8
    c. 3
    d. 3.5

17. A goat eats 214 kg. of hay in 60 days, while a cow eats the same amount in 15 days. How long will it take to eat this hay together?

    a. 37.5
    b. 75
    c. 12
    d. 15

18. Sarah weighs 25 pounds more than Tony. If together they weigh 205 pounds, how much does Sarah weigh approximately in kilograms? Assume 1 pound = 0.4535 kilograms

    a. 41
    b. 48
    c. 50
    d. 52

19. Ann went from point A to point B. At the same time, Peter went from point B to point A. In 6 hours, they met, and in 3 more hours, Peter reached B. How many hours did it take Ann to travel from A to B?

    a. 18
    b. 9
    c. 15
    d. 12

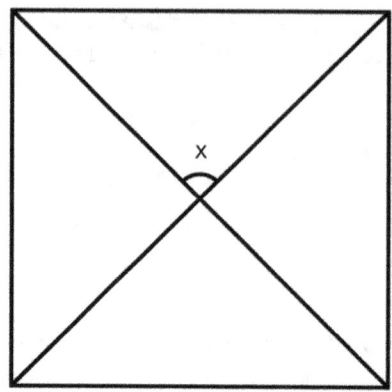

20. What is measurement of the indicated angle?

    a. 45°
    b. 90°
    c. 60°
    d. 30°

21. Mr. White wants to tile his rectangular backyard, which is 16 m × 11 m. The dimensions of each tile are 7 cm × 4 cm. If cost of each tile is $0.30 and 2.5% tiles break during handling, then what will be the total cost?

    a. $19234
    b. $20240
    c. $20895
    d. $21563

22. Translate the following into an equation: six times a number plus five.

    a. 6X + 5
    b. 6(X+5)
    c. 5X + 6
    d. (6 * 5) + 5

Mathematics

23. In the Euro cup football game, England won gold, Spain won silver and Holland won bronze medals. The three winners share the total prize money of $605,500 in the ratio of 4:2:1. How much money did Spain win?

    a. $86,500
    b. $173,000
    c. $201,830
    d. $346,000

24. Solve for b. $7 - 8b = 11 - 10b$.

    a. 2
    b. 3
    c. 5
    d. 6

25. A building is 15 m long and 20 m wide and 10 m high. What is the volume of the building?

    a. 45 m^3
    b. 3,000 m^3
    c. 1500 m^3
    d. 300 m^3

26. Solve 3/4 + 2/4 + 1.2

    a. 1 1/7
    b. 2 3/4
    c. 2 9/20
    d. 3 1/4

27. 3 boys are asked to clean a surface that is 4 ft². If the portion is divided equally among the boys, what size will each of them clean?

    a. 1 ft 6 inches

    b. 14 inches

    c. 1 ft 2 inches

    d. 1 ft² 48 in²

28. Great Britain has a Value Added Tax of 15%. A shop sells a camera for $545. If the VAT is included in the price, what is the actual cost of the camera?

    a. $490.40

    b. $473.91

    c. $505.00

    d. $503.15

29. Simplify 0.12 + 1 2/5 − 1 3/5

    a. 1 1/25

    b. -2/25

    c. 1 2/5

    d. 2 3/5

30. A rectangular box measures 10 cm long and 8 cm wide and 10 cm high. What is the volume of the box?

    a. 28 cm³

    b. 2000 cm³

    c. 400 cm³

    d. 800 cm³

Mathematics

31. 5 men have to share a load weighing 10 kg 550 g equally among themselves. How much weight will each man have to carry?

    a. 900 g
    b. 1.5 kg
    c. 3 kg
    d. 2 kg 110 g

32. A worker's weekly salary was increased by 30%. If his new salary is $150, what was his old salary?

    a. $120.00
    b. $99.15
    c. $109.00
    d. $115.38

33. Estimate 46,227 + 101,032.

    a. 14,700
    b. 147,000
    c. 14,700,000
    d. 104,700

34. 2/15 ÷ 4/5 =

    a. 6/65
    b. 6/75
    c. 5/12
    d. 1/6

35. If Tim deposits $5,500 in a savings account that offers a 5% interest, what will be the total amount in his savings account after 3 years?

    a. $6,225
    b. $6,0325
    c. $325
    d. $6,325

36. The price of a product was increased by 45%. If the initial cost was $220, what is the new cost?

    a. $230
    b. $300
    c. $319
    d. $245

37. A map uses a scale of 1:2,000. How much distance on the ground is 5.2 inches on the map if the scale is in inches?

    a. 100,400
    b. 10, 500
    c. 10,400
    d. 10,400

38. Find 2 numbers that sum to 21 and the sum of the squares is 261.

    a. 14 and 7
    b. 15 and 6
    c. 16 and 5
    d. 17 and 4

Mathematics

39. Susan wants to buy a leather jacket that costs $545.00 and is on sale for 10% off. What is the approximate cost?

    a. $525

    b. $450

    c. $475

    d. $500

40. Translate the following into an equation: Five greater than 3 times a number.

    a. 3X + 5

    b. 5X + 3

    c. (5 + 3)X

    d. 5(3 + X)

41. Richard gives 's' amount of salary to each of his 'n' employees weekly. If he has 'x' amount of money then how many days he can employ these 'n' employees.

    a. sx/7n

    b. 7x/nx

    c. nx/7s

    d. 7x/ns

42. A square box measures 20 cm long and 20 cm wide and 20 cm high. What is the volume of the box?

    a. 60 cm^3

    b. 20,000 cm^3

    c. 4,000 cm^3

    d. 8,000 cm^3

43. The owner of a pet store decided to increase the cost of all reptiles 45%. If the initial cost of a reptile was $220, what is the new cost?

    a. $230
    b. $300
    c. $290
    d. $245

44. A map uses a scale of 1:100,000. How much distance on the ground is 3 inches on the map if the scale is in inches?

    a. 13 inches
    b. 300,000 inches
    c. 30,000 inches
    d. 333.999 inches

45. What is 8 more than 2/5 of 20?

    a. 10
    b. 12
    c. 16
    d. 8

Mathematics

Answer Key

1. C
Total no. of balls = 10, number of yellow balls = 2, so, 2/10 X 100 = 20%

2. C
Area of the square = 12 × 12 = 144 cm². Let x be the width so 2x will be the length of rectangle. The area will be 2 x 2 and the perimeter will be 2(2x + x) = 6x. According to the condition 2 x 2 = 144 then x = 8.48 cm. The perimeter will be 6 × 8.48 = 50.88 = 51 cm.

3. B
There are 50 balls in the basket now. Let x be the yellow balls that are to be added to make it 65%. So the equation becomes X + 15 /X + 50 = 65/100. X = 50.

4. A
5000 X 4% = 200
5000 + 200 = $5200

5. C
Total weight of 13 students with average 42 will be = 42 * 13 = 546 kg.

The total weight of the remaining 2 will be found by subtracting the total weight of 13 students from the total weight of 15 students: 640.5 - 546 = 94.5 kg.

94.5 = the total weight of two students. One of these students weigh 48 kg, so;

The weight of the other will be = 94.5 − 48 = 46.5 kg

6. C
Total expense is $2000 and we are informed that $5 is spent per meter. Combining these two information, we know that the total length of the fence is 2000/5 = 400 meters.

The fence is built around a square-shaped field. If one side of the square is "a," the perimeter of the square is "4a." Here, the perimeter is equal to 400 meters. So,

400 = 4a

100 = a -> this means that one side of the square is equal to 100 meters

7. D
To convert to percent, simply multiply the decimal by 100 or move the decimal point 2 places to the right. Therefore, 23.67 x 100 = 2367%

8. C
144 ÷ 36 = 4

9. C
125: 500 is the same as 25 : 100 or 1 : 4. So the amount of salt will be 0.75/4 = 0.1875, or about .19 grams.

10. A
$200 invested at 15% per year will yield $30 interest at the end of the first year. For the second year, the interest will be 34.50, so it will take about 1 1/2 years before he can buy the bike.

11. D
Perimeter of triangle ABC is asked.

Perimeter of a triangle = sum of the three sides.

Here, Perimeter of ΔABC = |AC| + |CB| + |AB|.

Since the triangle is located in the middle of two adjacent and identical rectangles, we find the side lengths using these rectangles:

|AB| = 6 + 6 = 12 cm

|CB| = 8.5 cm

|AC| = |CB| = 8.5 cm

Perimeter = |AC| + |CB| + |AB| = 8.5 + 8.5 + 12 = 29 cm

Mathematics

12. A
19304.56 − 5284.34 − 8384.76 = 5635.46

13. A
Let us first mention the money Tony spent: $80

Now we need to find the money Tony earned:

He had 15 dozen eggs = 15 * 12 = 180 eggs. 16 eggs were broken. So,

Remaining number of eggs that Tony sold = 180 − 16 = 164.

Total amount he earned for selling 164 eggs = 164 * 0.54 = $88.56.

As a summary, he spent $80 and earned $88.56.

The profit is the difference: 88.56 - 80 = $8.56

Percentage profit is found by proportioning the profit to the money he spent:

8.56 * 100/80 = 10.7%

Checking the answers, we round 10.7 to the nearest whole number: 11%

14. D
Let the original price = x,
80/100 = 12590/X,
80X = 1259000,
X = 15737.50.

15. C
16 X 230 = 3680, or about 3100.

16. C
Let X = total number of families
Y = total number of children
Y = 9 x 3 + 8 x 2 + 4 x 5 = 63 and
X = 9 + 8 + 4 = 21
Average number of children in a family = Y/X = 63/21 = 3

17. C
Total hay = 214 kg,
The goat eats at a rate of 214/60 days = 3.6 kg per day.
The cow eats at a rate of 214/15 = 14.3 kg per day,
Together they eat 3.6 + 14.3 = 17.9 per day.
At a rate of 17.9 kg per day, they will consume 214 kg in 214/17.9 = 11.96 or 12 days approx.

18. D
Let us denote Sarah's weight by "x." Then, since she weighs 25 pounds more than Tony, Tony will be x-25. They together weigh 205 pounds which means that the sum of the two representations will be equal to 205:

Sarah : x

Tony : x - 25

x + (x - 25) = 205 ... by arranging this equation we have:

x + x - 25 = 205

2x - 25 = 205 ... we add 25 to each side to have x term alone:

2x - 25 + 25 = 205 + 25

2x = 230

x = 230/2

x = 115 pounds -> Sarah weighs 115 pounds. Since 1 pound is 0.4535 kilograms, we need to multiply 115 by 0.4535 to have her weight in kilograms:

x = 115 * 0.4535 = 52.1525 kilograms -> this is equal to 52 when rounded to the nearest whole number.

Mathematics

19. D
It took peter 3 hours to cover the distance Ann traveled in 6 hours (from point of meeting to point A, where Ann started). This means Peter is traveling at twice the speed of Ann. If it took peter 6 hours to reach the point of meeting, it will take Ann twice that long to get to Peter's point of origin = 6 x 2 = 12

20. A
The diagonals of a square intersect at right angles, so each angle measures 90° Half of that angle will be 45°

21. A
The area of each tile is 7 cm X 4 cm = 28 cm². The area of the yard is 16 m X 11 m = 176 m² = 1760000 cm². The number of tiles required is 1760000/28 = 62858. 2% of the tiles break during handling, so 1.02 X 62858 = 64115. Total cost will be 64115 X 0.3 = $19234.55.

22. B
Six times a number plus five is the same as saying six times (a number plus five). Or, 6 * (a number plus five). Let X be the number so, 6(X+5).

23. B
Spain won second prize so their ratio is 2/7
2/7 * 60550 = $173,000

24. A
7 – 8b = 11 – 10b. Bring same terms to same side of the equation by changing the negative or positive signs when they cross over, therefore -8b + 10b = 11 – 7, 2b = 4, b = 4/2 = 2

25. B
Formula for volume of a shape is L x W x H = 15 x 20 x 10 = 3,000 m³

26. C
3/4 + 2/4 + 1.2, first convert the decimal to fraction, = 3/4 + 2/4 + 1 1/5 = ¾ + 2/4 + 6/5 = (find common denominator) (15 + 10 + 24)/20 = 49/20 = 2 9/20

27. D
1 foot is equal to 12 inches. So 1 ft² = 12 * 12 in²
4 ft² = 4 * 12 * 12 in² = 576 in²

The total surface area is divided equally among 3 boys.

Each boy will clean 576/3 = 192 in²

192 in² = 144 in² + 48 in²; 144 in² = 1 ft²

So, each boy will clean 1 ft² and 48 in²

28. B
Actual cost = X, therefore, 545 = x + 0.15x, 545 = 1x + 0.15x, 545 = 1.15x, x = 545/1.15 = 473.91

29. B
0.12 + 2/5 + 3a/5, Convert decimal to fraction to get 3/25 + 2/5 + 3/5, = (3 + 10 + 15)/25, = 28/25 = 1 3/25

30. D
Formula for volume of a shape is L x W x H = 10 x 8 x 10 = 800 cm³

31. D
First convert the unit of measurements to be the same. Since 1000 g = 1 kg, 10 kg = 10 x 1000 = 10,000 + 550 g = 10,550 g. Divide 10,550 among 5 = 10550/5 = 2110 = 2 kg 110 g

32. D
Let old salary = X, therefore $150 = x + 0.30x, 150 = 1x + 0.30x, 150 = 1.30x, x = 150/1.30 = 115.38
33. B
46,227 + 101,032 is approximately 147,000. The actual total is 147,259.
34. D
To divide fractions, multiply the first fraction with the inverse of the second fraction. 2/15 x 5/4, (cancel out) = 1/3 x 1/2 = 1/6

35. D
P = $5,500, t = 3 years, r = 5%, I = ? convert rate to deci-

mal and 5% = 0.05
I = 5,500 x 0.05 x 3 = 825. Total amount in the account = principal + interest or 5,500 + 825 = $6,325

36. C
Initial cost was $220. new cost = 220 + 45% of 220,
45/100 x 220 = 99, therefore new price is 220 + 99 = $319.

37. C
1 inch on map = 2,000 inches on ground. So, 5.2 inches on map = 5.2 * 2,000 = 10,400 inches on ground.

38. B
The numbers are 15 and 6.
$x + 7 = 21 \Rightarrow x = 21 - 7$
$x^2 + y^2 = 261$

$(21 - 7)^2 + y^2 = 261$
$441 - 42y + y^2 + y^2 = 261$
$2y^2 - 42y + 180 = 0$
$y^2 - 21y + 90 = 0$
$y_{1,2} = 21 \pm \sqrt{441 - 360}/2$
$y_{1,2} = 21 \pm \sqrt{81}/2$
$y_{1,2} = 21 \pm 9/2$
$y_1 = 15$
$y_2 = 6$
$x_1 = 21 - y_1 = 21 - 15 = 6$
$x_2 = 21 - y_2 = 21 - 6 = 15$

39. D
The jacket costs $545.00 so we can round up to $550. 10% of $550 is 55. We can round down to $50, which is easier to work with.

$550 - $50 is $500. The jacket will cost about $500.

The actual cost will be 10% X 545 = $54.50

545 – 54.50 = $490.50

40. A
Five greater than 3 times a number.
5 + 3 times a number.
3X + 5

41. D
We understand that each of the n employees earn s amount of salary weekly. This means that one employee earns s salary weekly. So; Richard has ns amount of money to employ n employees for a week.

We are asked to find the number of days n employees can be employed with x amount of money. We can do simple direct proportion:

If Richard can employ n employees for 7 days with ns amount of money,

Richard can employ n employees for y days with x amount of money ... y is the number of days we need to find.

We can do cross multiplication:

y = (x * 7)/(ns)

y = 7x/ns

42. D
Formula for volume of a shape is L x W x H = 20 x 20 x 20 = 8,000 cm^3

43. C. Initial cost was $200. New cost = 200 + 45% of 200, 45% of 200, 45/100 x 200 = 90, therefore new price is 200 + 90 = $290

44. B
1 inch on map = 100,000 inches on ground. So 3 inches on map = 3 x 100,000 = 300,000 inches on ground

45. C
2/5 of 20 = 8 + 8 = 16

Mathematics *143*

Fraction Tips, Tricks and Short-cuts

When you are writing an exam, time is precious, so anything you can do to answer questions faster is a real advantage.

Here are some ideas, Short-cuts, tips and tricks that can speed up answering fraction problems.

Remember that a fraction is just a number which names a portion of something. For instance, instead of having a whole pie, a fraction says you have a part of a pie--such as a half of one or a fourth of one.

Two numbers make up a fraction. The number on top is the numerator. The number on the bottom is the denominator.

To remember which is which, just remember that "denominator" and "down" both start with a "d." And the "downstairs" number is the denominator. So for instance, in ½, the numerator is 1, and the denominator (or "downstairs") number is 2.

Adding Fractions

It's easy to add two fractions if they have the same denominator. Just add the digits on top and leave the bottom one the same: 1/10 + 6/10 = 7/10.

It's the same with subtracting fractions with the same denominator: 7/10 - 6/10 = 1/10.

Adding and subtracting fractions with different denominators is a little more complicated.

First, you have to arrange the fractions so they have the same denominators.

The easiest way to do this is to multiply the denominators: For 2/5 + 1/2 multiply 5 by 2. Now you have a denominator of 10.

But now you have to change the top numbers too. Since you multiplied the 5 in 2/5 by 2, you also multiply the 2 by 2, to get 4. So the first fraction is now 4/10.

In the second fraction, you multiplied the denominator by 5, you have to multiply the numerator by 5 also, to get 5/10.

Now you have 4/10 + 5/10 and you can add 5 and 4 to get 9/10.

Simplest Form

To reduce a fraction to its simplest form, you have to arrange the numerator and denominator so the only common factor is 1.

Think of it this way:

Let's take an example: The fraction 2/10.

This is not reduced to its simplest terms because there is a number that will divide evenly into both: 2. We want to make it so that the only number that will divide evenly into both is 1.
Divide the top and bottom by 2 to get the new, reduced fraction - 1/5.

Multiplying Fractions

This is the easiest of all: Just multiply the two top numbers and then multiply the two bottom numbers.

Here is an example,

2/5 X 2/3

First, multiply the numerators: 2 X 2 = 4

then multiply the denominators: 5 X 3 = 15

Your answer is 4/15.

Mathematics

Dividing Fractions

Dividing fractions is easy if you remember a simple trick - first turn the second fraction upside down - then multiply!

Here is an example:

7/8 X 1/2

Turn the second fraction upside down:

7/8 X 2/1

then multiply:

(7 X 2) / (8 X 1) = 14/8

Converting Fractions to Decimals

There are a couple of ways to convert fractions to decimals. The first, which is the fastest -- is to memorize some basic fraction facts.

1/100 is "one hundredth," expressed as a decimal, it's .01.

1/50 is "two hundredths," expressed as a decimal, it's .02.

1/25 is "one twenty-fifth" or "four hundredths," expressed as a decimal, it's .04.

1/20 is "one twentieth" or ""five hundredths," expressed as a decimal, it's .05.

1/10 is "one tenth," expressed as a decimal, it's .1.

1/8 is "one eighth," or "one hundred twenty-five thousandths," expressed as a decimal, it's .125.

1/5 is "one fifth," or "two tenths," expressed as a decimal, it's .2.

1/4 is "one fourth" or "twenty-five hundredths," expressed as a decimal, it's .25.

1/3 is "one third" or "thirty-three hundredths," expressed as a decimal, it's .33.

1/2 is "one half" or "five tenths," expressed as a decimal, it's .5.

3/4 is "three fourths," or "seventy-five hundredths," expressed as a decimal, it's .75.

Of course, if you're no good at memorization, another good technique for converting a fraction to a decimal is to manipulate it so that the fraction's denominator is 10, 100, 1000, or some other power of 10.

Here's an example: We'll start with three quarters. What is the first number in the 4 "times table" that you can multiply and get a multiple of 10? Can you multiply 4 by something to get 10? No. Can you multiply it by something to get 100? Yes! 4 X 25 is 100.

So multiply the numerator by 25, which is 75 over 100

We know fractions are really a division problem, and we also know that dividing by 100, means we move the decimal 2 places to the left.

So, 75 over 100 = .75

Lets try another example - Convert one fifth to a decimal.

First find a power of 10 that 5 goes into evenly, which is 2.

Multiply the numerator and denominator by 2, which is

two tenths.

Dividing 2 by 10 means we move the decimal place 1 place to the left.

So 1/5 = 0.5

Mathematics

Converting Fractions to Percent

Here is a quick method to convert fraction to percent and a strategy for answering on a multiple choice test that will save you valuable exam time.

First, remember that a fraction is a division problem: you're dividing the bottom number into the top.

Taking an example, convert 2/3 into percent.

The first method is to multiple the numerator by 100 and divide. So,

(2 X 100) / 2 = 100/3 = 66.66

Add a % sign and you have the answer, 66.66%

If you're doing these conversions on a multiple-choice test, here's an idea that might be even easier and faster. Let's say you have a fraction of 1/8 and you're asked to convert to percent.

Since we know that "percent" means hundredths, ask yourself what number we can multiply 8 by to get 100. Since there is no number, ask what number gets us close to 100.

That number is 12: 8 X 12 = 96. So it gets us a little less than 100. Now, whatever you do to the denominator, you have to do to the numerator. Let's multiply 1 X 12 and we get 12. However, since 96 is a little less than 100, we know that our answer will be a little MORE than 12%.

Look at the choices and eliminate the obvious wrong choices. So if your possible answers on the multiple-choice test are these:

a) 8.5% b) 19% c)12.5% d) 25%

then we know the answer is c) 12.5%, because it's a little

MORE than the 12 we got in our math problem above.

Here all the choices except choice C 12.5% can be eliminated.

You don't have to know the exact correct answer, just enough to estimate, then eliminate the obviously wrong answers.

This was an easy example to demonstrate the strategy, but don't be fooled! You probably won't get such an easy question on your exam. By estimating your answer quickly, then eliminating obviously incorrect choices immediately, you save precious exam time.

Decimal Tips, Tricks and Short-cuts

Converting Decimals to Fractions

Converting decimals to fractions is easy if you say it the right way! If you say "point one" or "point 25," you'll have trouble.

But if you say, "one tenth" and "twenty-five hundredths," then you have already solved it! That's because, if you know your fractions, you know that "one tenth" looks like this: 1/10. And "twenty-five hundredths" looks like this: 25/100.

Even if you have digits before the decimal, such as 3.4, learning how to say the word will help you with the conversion into a fraction. It's not "three point four," it's "three and four tenths." Knowing this, you know that the fraction which looks like "three and four tenths" is 3 4/10.

The conversion is not complete until you reduce the fraction to its lowest terms: It's not 25/100, but 1/4.

Mathematics

Converting Decimals to Percent

Changing a decimal to a percent is easy if you remember one thing: multiply by 100.

For example, if you start with .45, simply multiply it by 100 for 45. Then add the % sign to the end - 45%.

Think of it this way: take out the decimal point, add a percent sign on the opposite side. In other words, the decimal on the left is replaced by the % on the right.

It doesn't work quite that easily if the decimal is in the middle of the number. For example, 3.7. Here, take out the decimal in the middle and replace it with a 0 % at the end. So 3.7 converted to decimal is 370%.

Percent Tips, Tricks and Short-cuts

Percent problems are not nearly as scary as they appear, if you remember this neat trick:

Draw a cross as in:

Portion	Percent
Whole	100

In the upper left, write PORTION. In the bottom left write WHOLE. In the top right, write PERCENT and in the bottom right, write 100. Whatever your problem is, you will leave blank the unknown, and fill in the other four parts. For example, let's suppose your problem is: Find 10% of 50. Since we know the 10% part, we put 10 in the percent corner. Since the whole number in our problem is 50, we put that in the corner marked whole. You always put 100 underneath the percent, so we leave it as is, which leaves only the top left corner blank. This is where we'll put our answer. Now simply multiply the two corner numbers that are NOT 100. Here, it's 10 X 50. That gives us 500. Now divide this by the remaining corner, or 100, to get a final answer of 5. 5 is the number that goes in the upper-left corner, and is your final solution.

Another hint to remember: Percents are the same thing as hundredths in decimals. So .45 is the same as 45 hundredths or 45 percent.

Converting Percents to Decimals

Percents are just a type of decimal, so it should be no surprise that converting between the two is actually fairly simple. Here are a few tricks and Short-cuts to keep in mind:

- Remember that percent literally means "per 100" or "for every 100." So when you speak of 30% you're saying 30 for every 100 or the fraction 30/100. In basic math, you learned that fractions that have 10 or 100 as the denominator can easily be turned to a decimal. 30/100 is thirty hundredths, or expressed as a decimal, .30.
- Another way to look at it: To convert a percent to a decimal, simply divide the number by 100. So for instance, if the percent is 47%, divide 47 by 100. The result will be .47. Get rid of the % mark and you're done.
- Remember that the easiest way of dividing by 100 is by moving your decimal two spots to the left.

Mathematics

Converting Percents to Fractions

Converting percents to fractions is easy. After all, a percent is just a type of fraction; it tells you what part of 100 that you're talking about. Here are some simple ideas for making the conversion from a percent to a fraction:

- If the percent is a whole number -- say 34% -- then simply write a fraction with 100 as the denominator (the bottom number). Then put the percentage itself on top. So 34% becomes 34/100.
- Now reduce as you would reduce any percent. In this case, by dividing 2 into 34 and 2 into 100, you get 17/50.
- If your percent is not a whole number -- say 3.4% --then convert it to a decimal expressed as hundredths. 3.4 is the same as 3.40 (or 3 and forty hundredths). Now ask yourself how you would express "three and forty hundredths" as a fraction. It would, of course, be 3 40/100. Reduce this and it becomes 3 2/5.

How to Answer Basic Math Questions - the Basics

First, read the problem, but not the answers.

Work through the problem first and come up with your own answers. Hopefully, you should find your answer among the choices.

If no answer matches the one you got, re-check your math, but this time, use a different method. In math, there are different ways to solve a problem.

Math Multiple Choice Strategy

The two strategies for working with basic math multiple choice are Estimation and Elimination.

Estimation is just as it sounds - try to estimate an approximate answer first. Then look at the choices.

Elimination is probably the most powerful strategy for answering multiple choice.

Eliminate obviously incorrect answers and narrowing the possible choices.

Here are a few basic math examples of how this works.

Solve 2/3 + 5/12

    a. 9/17

    b. 3/11

    c. 7/12

    d. 1 1/12

First estimate the answer. 2/3 is more than half and 5/12 is about half, so the answer is going to be very close to 1.

Next, Eliminate. Choice A is about 1/2 and can be eliminated, choice B is very small, less than 1/2 and can be eliminated. Choice C is close to 1/2 and can be eliminated. Leaving only choice D, which is just over 1.

Work through the solution, find a common denominator and add. The correct answer is 1 1/12, so Choice D is correct.

Mathematics

Let's look at another example:

Solve 4/5 – 2/3

    a. 2/2
    b. 2/13
    c. 1
    d. 2/15

First, quickly estimate the answer. 4/5 is very close to 1, and 2/3 more than half, so the answer is going to be less than 1/2.

Choice A can be eliminated right away, because it is 1. Choice C can be eliminated for the same reason.

Next, look at the denominators. Since 5 and 3 don't go into 13, choice B can be eliminated as well.

That leaves choice D. Checking the answer, the common denominator will be 15. So the answer is 2/15 and choice D is correct.

Fractions shortcut - Cancelling out

In any operation with fractions, if the numerator of one fractions has a common multiple with the denominator of the other, you can cancel out. This saves time, and simplifies the problem quickly, making it easier to manage.

Solve 2/15 ÷ 4/5

    a. 6/65
    b. 6/75
    c. 5/12
    d. 1/6

To divide fractions, we multiply the first fraction with the inverse of the second fraction. Therefore we have 2/15 x 5/4. The numerator of the first fraction, 2, shares a multiple with the denominator of the second fraction, 4, which is 2. These cancel out, which gives, 1/3 x 1/2 = 1/6

Cancelling out solved the questions very quickly, but we can still use multiple choice strategies to answer.

Choice B can be eliminated because 75 is too large a denominator. Choice C can be eliminated because 5 and 15 don't go into 12.

Choice D is correct.

Decimal Multiple Choice Strategy and Short-cuts.

Multiplying decimals gives a very quick way to estimate and eliminate choices. Anytime that you multiply decimals, it is going to give an answer with the same number of decimal places as the combined operands.

So for example,

2.38 X 1.2 will produce a number with three places of decimal, which is 2.856.

Here are a few examples with step-by-step explanation:

Solve 2.06 x 1.2

    a. 24.82

    b. 2.482

    c. 24.72

    d. 2.472

This is a simple question, but even before you start calculating, you can eliminate several choices. When multiplying decimals, there will always be as many numbers behind the decimal place in the answer as the sum of the ones in the initial problem, so choices A and C can be eliminated.

The correct answer is D: 2.06 x 1.2 = 2.472

Mathematics

Solve 20.0 ÷ 2.5

    a. 12.05

    b. 9.25

    c. 8.3

    d. 8

First estimate the answer to be around 10, and eliminate choice A. And since it'd also be an even number, you can eliminate Choices B and C, leaving only choice D.

The correct answer is choice D: 20.0 ÷ 2.5 = 8

How to Solve Word Problems

Do you know what the biggest tip for solving word problems is?

Practice regularly and systematically.

Sounds simple and easy right? Yes it is, and yes it really does work.

Word problems are a way of thinking and require you to translate a real-world problem into mathematical terms.

Some math teachers say that learning how to think mathematically is the main reason for teaching word problems.

So what does that mean?

Studying word problems and math in general requires a logical and mathematical frame of mind. The only way you can get this is by practicing regularly, which means every day.

It is critical that you practice word problems every day for the 5 days before the exam as the absolute minimum.

If you practice and miss a day, you have lost the mathematical frame of mind and the benefit of your previous practice is gone. You must start all over again.

Everything is important.

All the information given in the problem has some purpose. There is no unnecessary information! Word problems are typically around 50 words in 2 or 3 sentences.

Often, the relationships are complicated. To explain everything, every word counts.

Make sure that you use every piece of information.

Here are 9 simple steps to solve word problems.

Step 1 – Read through the problem at least three times. The first reading should be a quick scan, and the next two readings should be done slowly with a view to finding answers to these important questions:

What does the problem ask? (Usually located towards the end of the problem)

What does the problem imply? (This is usually a point you were asked to remember).

Mark all information, and underline all important words or phrases.

Step 2 – Try to make a pictorial representation of the problem such as a circle and an arrow to indicate travel. This makes the problem a bit more real and sensible to you.

A favorite word problem is something like, 1 train leaves Station A travelling at 100 km/hr and another train leaves Station B travelling at 60 km/hr. ...

Draw a line, the two stations, and the two trains at either end. This will help solidify the situation in your mind.

Step 3 – Use the information you have to make a table with a blank portion to indicate information you do not know.

Step 4 – Assign a single letter to represent each unknown data in your table. You can write down the unknown that each letter represents so that you do not make the error of assigning answers to the wrong unknown, because a word problem may have multiple unknowns and you will need to create equations for each unknown.

Step 5 – Translate the English terms in the word problem into a mathematical algebraic equation. Remember that the main problem with word problems is that they are not expressed in regular math equations. You ability to correctly identify the variables and translate the word problem into an equation determines your ability to solve the problem.

Step 6 – Check the equation to see if it looks like regular equations that you are used to seeing and whether it looks sensible. Does the equation appear to represent the information in the question? Take note that you may need to rewrite some formulas needed to solve the word problem equation. For example, word distance problems may need you rewriting the distance formula, which is Distance = Time x Rate. If the word problem requires that you solve for time you will need to use Distance/Rate and Distance/Time to solve for Rate. If you understand the distance word problem you should be able to identify the variable you need to solve for.

Step 7 – Use algebra rules to solve the derived equation. Take note that the laws of equation demands that what is done on this side of the equation has to also be done on the other side. You have to solve the equation so that the unknown ends up alone on one side. Where there are multiple unknowns you will need to use elimination or substitution methods to resolve all the equations.

Step 8 – Check your final answers to see if they make sense with the information given in the problem. For example if the word problem involves a discount, the final price should be less or if a product was taxed then the final answer has to cost more.

Step 9 – Cross check your answers by placing the answer or answers in the first equation to replace the unknown or unknowns. If your answer is correct then both side of the equation must equate or equal. If your answer is not correct then you may have derived a wrong equation or solved the equation wrongly. Repeat the necessary steps to correct.

Types of Word Problems

Word problems can be classified into 12 types. Below are examples of each type with a complete solution. Some types of word problems can be solved quickly using multiple choice strategies and some cannot. Always look for ways to estimate the answer and then eliminate choices.

1. Age

A girl is 10 years older than her brother. By next year, she will be twice the age of her brother. What are their ages now?

    a. 25, 15
    b. 19, 9
    c. 21, 11
    d. 29, 19

Solution: B

We will assume that the girl's age is "a" and her brother's age is "b." This means that based on the information in the first sentence,
$a = 10 + b$

Next year, she will be twice her brother's age, which gives,
$a + 1 = 2(b + 1)$

Mathematics

We need to solve for one unknown factor and then use the answer to solve for the other. To do this we substitute the value of "a" from the first equation into the second equation. This gives

$10 + b + 1 = 2b + 2$
$11 + b = 2b + 2$
$11 - 2 = 2b - b$
$b = 9$

$9 = b$ this means that her brother is 9 years old. Solving for the girl's age in the first equation gives $a = 10 + 9$. $a = 19$ the girl is aged 19. So, the girl is aged 19 and the boy is 9

2. Distance or speed

Two boats travel down a river towards the same destination, starting at the same time. One boat is traveling at 52 km/hr, and the other boat at 43 km/hr. How far apart will they be after 40 minutes?

   a. 46.67 km
   b. 19.23 km
   c. 6.04 km
   d. 14.39 km

Solution: C

After 40 minutes, the first boat will have traveled = 52 km/hr x 40 minutes/60 minutes = 34.66 km
After 40 minutes, the second boat will have traveled = 43 km/hr x 40/60 minutes = 28.66 km
Difference between the two boats will be 34.66 km – 28.66 km = 6 km.

Multiple Choice Strategy

First estimate the answer. The first boat is travelling 9 km. faster than the second, for 40 minutes, which is 2/3 of an hour. 2/3 of 9 = 6, as a rough guess of the distance apart.

Choices A, B and D can be eliminated right away.

3. Ratio

The instructions in a cookbook state that 700 grams of flour must be mixed in 100 ml of water, and 0.90 grams of salt added. A cook however has just 325 grams of flour. What is the quantity of water and salt that he should use?

      a. 0.41 grams and 46.4 ml
      b. 0.45 grams and 49.3 ml
      c. 0.39 grams and 39.8 ml
      d. 0.25 grams and 40.1 ml

Solution: A

The Cookbook states 700 grams of flour, but the cook only has 325. The first step is to determine the percentage of flour he has 325/700 x 100 = 46.4%
That means that 46.4% of all other items must also be used.
46.4% of 100 = 46.4 ml of water
46.4% of 0.90 = 0.41 grams of salt.

Multiple Choice Strategy

The recipe calls for 700 grams of flour but the cook only has 325, which is just less than half, the quantity of water and salt are going to be about half.

Choices C and D can be eliminated right away. Choice B is very close so be careful. Looking closely at Choice B, it is exactly half, and since 325 is slightly less than half of 700, it can't be correct.

Choice A is correct.

Mathematics

4. Percent

An agent received $6,685 as his commission for selling a property. If his commission was 13% of the selling price, how much was the property?

  a. $68,825
  b. $121,850
  c. $49,025
  d. $51,423

Solution: D

Let's assume that the property price is x
That means from the information given, 13% of x = 6,685
Solve for x,
x = 6685 x 100/13 = $51,423

Multiple Choice Strategy

The commission, 13%, is just over 10%, which is easier to work with. Round up $6685 to $6700, and multiple by 10 for an approximate answer. 10 X 6700 = $67,000. You can do this in your head. Choice B is much too big and can be eliminated. Choice C is too small and can be eliminated. Choices A and D are left and good possibilities.

Do the calculations to make the final choice.

5. Sales & Profit

A store owner buys merchandise for $21,045. He transports them for $3,905 and pays his staff $1,450 to stock the merchandise on his shelves. If he does not incur further costs, how much does he need to sell the items to make $5,000 profit?

  a. $32,500
  b. $29,350
  c. $32,400
  d. $31,400

Solution: D

Total cost of the items is $21,045 + $3,905 + $1,450 = $26,400
Total cost is now $26,400 + $5000 profit = $31,400

Multiple Choice Strategy

Round off and add the numbers up in your head quickly. 21,000 + 4,000 + 1500 = 26500. Add in 5000 profit for a total of 31500.

Choice B is too small and can be eliminated. Choices C and A are too large and can be eliminated.

6. Tax/Income

A woman earns $42,000 per month and pays 5% tax on her monthly income. If the Government increases her monthly taxes by $1,500, what is her income after tax?

    a. $38,400
    b. $36,050
    c. $40,500
    d. $39, 500

Solution: A

Initial tax on income was 5/100 x 42,000 = $2,100
$1,500 was added to the tax to give $2,100 + 1,500 = $3,600
Income after tax is $42,000 - $3,600 = $38,400

7. Simple Interest Word Problems

Simple interest is one type of interest problems. There are always four variables of any simple interest equation. With simple interest, you would be given three of these variables and be asked to solve for one unknown variable. With more complex interest problems, you would have to solve for multiple variables.

The four variables of simple interest are:
P – Principal which refers to the original amount of money

Mathematics

put in the account
I – Interest or the amount of money earned as interest
r – Rate or interest rate. This MUST ALWAYS be in decimal format and not in percentage
t – Time or the amount of time the money is kept in the account to earn interest

The formula for simple interest is I = P x r x t

Example 1

A customer deposits $1,000 in a savings account with a bank that offers 2% interest. How much interest will be earned after 4 years?
For this problem, there are 3 variables as expected.

P = $1,000
t = 4 years
r = 2%
I = ?

Before we can begin solving for I using the simple interest formula, we need to first convert the rate from percentage to decimal.

2% = 2/100 = 0.02

Now we can use the formula: I = P x r x t

I = 1,000 x 0.02 x 4 = 80
This means that the $1,000 would have earned an interest of $80 after 4 years. The total in the account after 4 years will thus be principal + interest earned, or 1,000 + 80 = $1,080

Example 2

Sandra deposits $1400 in a savings account with a bank at 5% interest. How long will she have to leave the money in the bank to earn $420 as interest to buy a second-hand car?

In this example, the given information is:
I = $420
P = $1,400
r - 5%
t - ?

As usual, first we convert the rate from percentage to decimal
5% = 5/100 = 0.05

Next, we plug in the variables we know into the simple interest formula - I = P x r x t

420 = 1,400 x 0.05 x t
420 = 70 x t
420 = 70t
t = 420/70
t = 6

Sandra will have to leave her $1,400 in the bank for 6 years to earn her an interest of $420 at a rate of 5%.

Other important simple interest formula to remember

To use this formula below, do not convert r (rate) to decimal.

P = 100 x interest/ r x t
r = 100 x interest/p x t
t = 100 x interest/ p x r

8. Averaging

The average weight of 10 books is 54 grams. 2 more books were added and the average weight became 55.4. If one of the 2 new books added weighed 62.8 g, what is the weight of the other?

    a. 44.7 g
    b. 67.4 g
    c. 62 g
    d. 52 g

Mathematics

Solution: C

Total weight of 10 books with average 54 grams will be = 10 × 54 = 540 g
Total weight of 12 books with average 55.4 will be = 55.4 × 12 = 664.8 g
So total weight of the remaining 2 will be= 664.8 − 540 = 124.8 g
If one weighs 62.8, the weight of the other will be= 124.8 g − 62.8 g = 62 g

Multiple Choice Strategy

Averaging problems can be estimated by looking at which direction the average goes. If additional items are added and the average goes up, the new items much be greater than the average. If the average goes down after new items are added, the new items must be less than the average.

Here, the average is 54 grams and 2 books are added which increases the average to 55.4, so the new books must weight more than 54 grams.
Choices A and D can be eliminated right away.

9. Probability

A bag contains 15 marbles of various colors. If 3 marbles are white, 5 are red and the rest are black, what is the probability of randomly picking out a black marble from the bag?

   a. 7/15
   b. 3/15
   c. 1/5
   d. 4/15

Solution: A

Total marbles = 15
Number of black marbles = 15 − (3 + 5) = 7
Probability of picking out a black marble = 7/15

10. Two Variables

A company paid a total of $2850 to book for 6 single rooms and 4 double rooms in a hotel for one night. Another company paid $3185 to book for 13 single rooms for one night in the same hotel. What is the cost for single and double rooms in that hotel?

    a. single= $250 and double = $345
    b. single= $254 and double = $350
    c. single = $245 and double = $305
    d. single = $245 and double = $345

Solution: D

We can determine the price of single rooms from the information given of the second company. 13 single rooms = 3185.
One single room = 3185 / 13 = 245
The first company paid for 6 single rooms at $245. 245 x 6 = $1470
Total amount paid for 4 double rooms by first company = $2850 - $1470 = $1380
Cost per double room = 1380 / 4 = $345

11. Geometry

The length of a rectangle is 5 in. more than its width. The perimeter of the rectangle is 26 in. What is the width and length of the rectangle?

    a. width = 6 inches, Length = 9 inches
    b. width = 4 inches, Length = 9 inches
    c. width =4 inches, Length = 5 inches
    d. width = 6 inches, Length = 11 inches

Solution: B

Formula for perimeter of a rectangle is 2(L + W)
p=26, so 2(L+W) = p
The length is 5 inches more than the width, so
2(w+5) + 2w = 26
2w + 10 + 2w = 26
2w + 2w = 26 - 10

Mathematics

4w = 16

W = 16/4 = 4 inches

L is 5 inches more than w, so L = 5 + 4 = 9 inches.

12. Totals and fractions

A basket contains 125 oranges, mangos and apples. If 3/5 of the fruits in the basket are mangos and only 2/5 of the mangos are ripe, how many ripe mangos are there in the basket?

    a. 30
    b. 68
    c. 55
    d. 47

Solution: A
Number of mangos in the basket is 3/5 x 125 = 75
Number of ripe mangos = 2/5 x 75 = 30

Basic Algebraic Equations

Algebra is a basic form of mathematics designed to define unknown quantities called variables. Variables in algebra are represented by letters, often x, y and z or a, b and c, and they are placed in equations alongside known quantities. An algebraic equation can be as simple as 2x=6 where simple division can tell us that x=6/2 or x = 3. Equations can also have variables on both sides such as 2x+3=8x. For this equation, we need to take more steps. First, subtracting 2x from both sides we get the equation 3=6x. From there it is again a simple matter of division to show that x=.5. The point of an equation is that it demonstrates that two distinct pieces of information have the same value. (It equates them.) Even though we do not know what 2x+3 is or what 8x is, we at least know that they are the same.

Pass the COOP!

There are three types of equalities in algebra. There are reflexive equalities that say x=x. There are symmetric equalities that say that if x=y then y=x as well. And there are transitive equalities that say that if x=y and y=z then x=z.

The definite number next to the variable in each equation is called its coefficient. A variable can always be thought of as having a coefficient; if there is no number next to it, the coefficient equals 1, and if it has a negative sign in front of it, the coefficient equals -1.

Often, algebra is presented as word problems and it is up to you to figure out the equation. For instance, a question might describe a hockey team that has 6 wins, 3 losses in regulation time and 1 loss in overtime over their last 10 games. It will then tell you that the team has 13 points (awarded for wins and overtime losses to organize the league's standings) in their last 10 games and ask, given that a regulation loss earns a team 0 points: How many points is a win worth? How many is an overtime loss worth?

This question will give you the variables x = a win, y = a regulation loss and z = an overtime loss, from which you can derive the equation 6x+3y+1z=13. Since you already know that y=0 points, you can rewrite the equation as 6x+z=13. Now we have a two variable or polynomial equation to solve. First, we need to find a way to rewrite it so that there is only one variable in the equation. If we solve for x we get the equation 6x=13-1z which can be simplified to x=2z. We can then plug that into the original equation and get 6(2z)+z=13 or 13z=13 or z=1. Now we know two variables that we can use to solve for x and we can write the equation 6x+1=13 or x=2. Thus, we can tell that in hockey teams get 2 points for each regulation win (x=2) and 1 point for each overtime win (z=1).

This is a highly simplified example of algebra, but the same process works with any basic mathematical function provided you follow the order of operations. The order of operations is the order in which you have to perform each mathematical function to get the correct answer. Following the order of operations is important because while some operations can be done in any order:

Mathematics

(1+2)+3 = 3+3 = 6 is the same as (2+3)+1 = 5+1 = 6

others cannot:

(10-2)/4 = 8/4 = 2 is not the same as (10/4)-2 = 2.5-2 = .5

Doing the operations in any order you want can give you very incorrect results.

The order of operations goes: parentheses, exponents, multiplication, division, addition, subtraction. It can be remembered through the acronym Please Excuse My Dear Aunt Sally.

Basic Geometry

To locate dots and draw lines and curves, we use the co-ordinate plane. It also called Cartesian coordinate plane. It is a two-dimensional surface with a coordinate grid in it, which helps us to count the units. For the counting of those units, we use x-axis (horizontal scale) and y-axis (vertical scale).

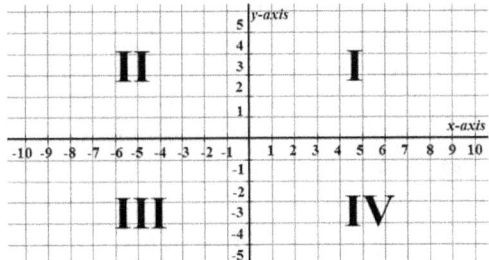

The whole system is called a coordinate system which is divided into 4 parts, called quadrants. The quadrant where all numbers are positive is the 1st quadrant (I), and if we go counterclockwise, we mark all 4 quadrants.

The location of a dot in the coordinate system is represented by coordinates. Coordinates are represented as a pair of numbers, where the 1st number is located on the x-axis and the 2nd number is located on the y-axis. So, if a dot A has coordinates a and b, then we write:

A=(a,b)   or   A(a,b)

The point where x-axis and y-axis intersect is called an origin. The origin is the point from which we measure the distance along the x and y axes.

In the Cartesian coordinate system we can calculate the distance between 2 given points. If we have dots with coordinates:
A=(a,b)
B=(c,d)

Then the distance d between A and B can be calculated by the following formula:

$$d = \sqrt{(c-a)^2 + (d-b)^2}$$

Cartesian coordinate system is used for the drawing of 2-dimentional shapes, and is also commonly used for functions.

Example:

Draw the function   y = (1 - x)/2

To draw a linear function, we need at least 2 points.
If we put that x=0 then value for y would be:

$$y = \frac{1-x}{2} = \frac{1-0}{2} = \frac{1}{2}$$

We found the 1st point, let's name it A, with following coordinates:

Mathematics

A = (0,1/2)

To find the 2nd point, we can put that x=1. In this case, the value for y would be:

$$y = \frac{1-x}{2} = \frac{1-1}{2} = \frac{0}{2} = 0$$

If we denote the 2nd point with B, then the coordinates for this point are:

B=(1,0)

Since we have 2 points necessary for the function, we find them in the coordinate system and we connect them with a line that represents the function,

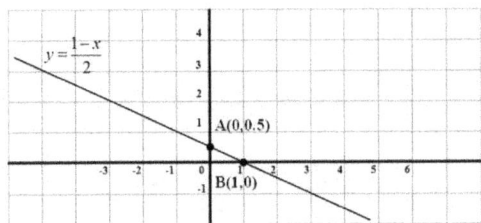

Perimeter Area and Volume

Perimeter and Area (2-dimentional shapes)

Perimeter of a shape determines the length around that shape, while the area includes the space inside the shape.

Rectangle:

$P = 2a + 2b$
$A = ab$

Square

$P = 4a$

$A = a^2$

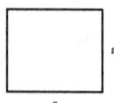

Parallelogram

$P = 2a + 2b$

$A = ah_a = bh_b$

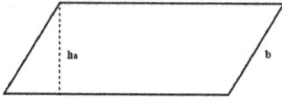

Rhombus

$P = 4a$

$A = ah = \dfrac{d_1 d_2}{2}$

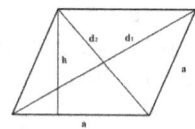

Equilateral Triangle

$P = 3a$

$A = \dfrac{a^2 \sqrt{3}}{4}$

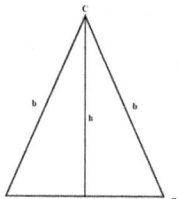

Trapezoid

$P = a + b + c + d$

$A = \dfrac{a+b}{2} h$

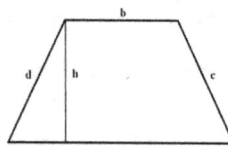

Circle

$P = 2r\pi$

$A = r^2 \pi$

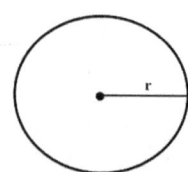

Mathematics

Area and Volume (3-dimentional shapes)

To calculate the area of a 3-dimentional shape, we calculate the areas of all sides and then we add them all.

To find the volume of a 3-dimentional shape, we multiply the area of the base (B) and the height (H) of the 3-dimentional shape.

$$V = BH$$

For a pyramid and a cone, the volume would be divided by 3.

$$V = BH/3$$

Here are some of the 3-dimentional shapes with formulas for their area and volume:

Cuboids

$A = 2(ab + bc + ac)$
$V = abc$

Cube

$A = 6a^2$
$V = a^3$

Pyramid

$A = ab + ah_a + bh_b$
$V = \dfrac{abH}{3}$

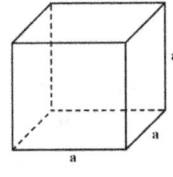

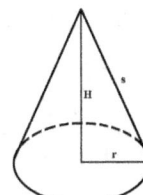

Cylinder

$$A = 2r^2\pi + 2r\pi H$$
$$V = r^2\pi H$$

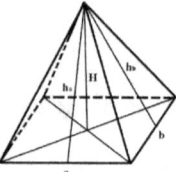

Cone

$$A = (r+s)r\pi$$
$$V = \frac{r^2\pi H}{3}$$

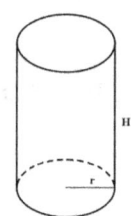

Pythagorean Geometry

If we have a right triangle ABC, where its sides (legs) are a and b and c is a hypotenuse (the side opposite the right angle), then we can establish a relationship between these sides using the following formula:

$$c^2 = a^2 + b^2$$

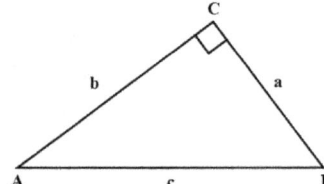

This formula is proven in the Pythagorean Theorem. There are many proofs of this theorem, but we'll look at just one geometrical proof:

If we draw squares on the right triangle's sides, then the area of the square upon the hypotenuse is equal to the sum of the areas of the squares that are upon other two sides of the triangle. Since the areas of these squares are a^2, b^2 and c^2, that is how we got the formula above.

Mathematics

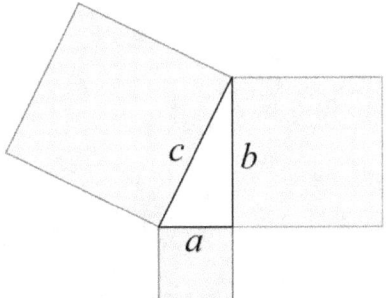

One of the famous right triangles is one with sides 3, 4 and 5. And we can see here that:

$3^2 + 4^2 = 5^2$
$9 + 16 = 25$
$25 = 25$

Example Problem:

The isosceles triangle ABC has a perimeter of 18 centimeters, and the difference between its base and legs is 3 centimeters. Find the height of this triangle.

We write the information we have about triangle ABC and we draw a picture of it for better understanding of the relation between its elements:

P=18 cm
a - b = 3 cm
h=?

We use the formula for the perimeter of the isosceles triangle, since that is what is given to us:

P=a+2b=18 cm

Notice that we have 2 equations with 2 variables, so we can solve it as a system of equations:

a + 2b = 18
a − b = 3 / a + 2b = 18

$2a - 2b = 6$ / $a + 2b + 2a - 2b = 18 + 6$
$3a = 24$
$a = 24/3 = 8$ cm

Now we go back to find b:
$a - b = 3$
$8 - b = 3$
$b = 8 - 3$
$b = 5$ cm

Using Pythagorean Theorem, we can find the height using a and b, because the height falls on the side a at the right angle. Notice that height cuts side a exactly in half, and that's why we use in the formula a/2. In this case, b is our hypotenuse, so we have:

$b^2 = (a/2)^2 + h^2$
$h^2 = b^2 - (a/2)^2$
$h^2 = 5^2 - (8/2)^2$
$h^2 = 5^2 - (8/2)^2$
$h^2 = 25 - 4^2$
$h^2 = 26 - 16$
$h^2 = 9$
$h = 3$ cm.

Practice Test Questions Set 1

THE PRACTICE TEST PORTION PRESENTS QUESTIONS THAT ARE REPRESENTATIVE OF THE TYPE OF QUESTION YOU SHOULD EXPECT TO FIND ON THE COOP. The questions below are not the same as you will find on the COOP - that would be too easy! And nobody knows what the questions will be and they change all the time. Below are general questions that cover the same areas as the COOP. So while the format and exact wording of the questions may differ slightly, and change from year to year, if you can answer the questions below, you will have no problem with the COOP.

For the best results, take this Practice Test as if it were the real exam. Set aside time when you will not be disturbed, and a location that is quiet and free of distractions. Read the instructions carefully, read each question carefully, and answer to the best of your ability.

Use the bubble answer sheets provided. When you have completed the Practice Test, check your answer against the Answer Key and read the explanation provided.

Section I – Sequences

Questions: 20
Time: 15 Minutes

Section II – Analogies

Questions: 20
Time: 7 Minutes

Section III – Quantitative and Verbal Reasoning

Questions: 40
Time: 30 Minutes

Section IV – Reading and Language Arts

Questions: 35
Time: 40 Minutes

Section V – Math

Questions: 40
Time: 40 Minutes

Practice Test Questions Set 1 179

Sequences

	A	B	C	D
1	○	○	○	○
2	○	○	○	○
3	○	○	○	○
4	○	○	○	○
5	○	○	○	○
6	○	○	○	○
7	○	○	○	○
8	○	○	○	○
9	○	○	○	○
10	○	○	○	○
11	○	○	○	○
12	○	○	○	○
13	○	○	○	○
14	○	○	○	○
15	○	○	○	○
16	○	○	○	○
17	○	○	○	○
18	○	○	○	○
19	○	○	○	○
20	○	○	○	○

Analogies

	A	B	C	D
1	○	○	○	○
2	○	○	○	○
3	○	○	○	○
4	○	○	○	○
5	○	○	○	○
6	○	○	○	○
7	○	○	○	○
8	○	○	○	○
9	○	○	○	○
10	○	○	○	○
11	○	○	○	○
12	○	○	○	○
13	○	○	○	○
14	○	○	○	○
15	○	○	○	○
16	○	○	○	○
17	○	○	○	○
18	○	○	○	○
19	○	○	○	○
20	○	○	○	○

Practice Test Questions Set 1

Quantitative & Verbal Reasoning

	A	B	C	D	E		A	B	C	D	E
1	○	○	○	○	○	21	○	○	○	○	○
2	○	○	○	○	○	22	○	○	○	○	○
3	○	○	○	○	○	23	○	○	○	○	○
4	○	○	○	○	○	24	○	○	○	○	○
5	○	○	○	○	○	25	○	○	○	○	○
6	○	○	○	○	○	26	○	○	○	○	○
7	○	○	○	○	○	27	○	○	○	○	○
8	○	○	○	○	○	28	○	○	○	○	○
9	○	○	○	○	○	29	○	○	○	○	○
10	○	○	○	○	○	30	○	○	○	○	○
11	○	○	○	○	○	31	○	○	○	○	○
12	○	○	○	○	○	32	○	○	○	○	○
13	○	○	○	○	○	33	○	○	○	○	○
14	○	○	○	○	○	34	○	○	○	○	○
15	○	○	○	○	○	35	○	○	○	○	○
16	○	○	○	○	○	36	○	○	○	○	○
17	○	○	○	○	○	37	○	○	○	○	○
18	○	○	○	○	○	38	○	○	○	○	○
19	○	○	○	○	○	39	○	○	○	○	○
20	○	○	○	○	○	40	○	○	○	○	○

Reading and Language Arts

	A	B	C	D	E		A	B	C	D	E
1	○	○	○	○	○	21	○	○	○	○	○
2	○	○	○	○	○	22	○	○	○	○	○
3	○	○	○	○	○	23	○	○	○	○	○
4	○	○	○	○	○	24	○	○	○	○	○
5	○	○	○	○	○	25	○	○	○	○	○
6	○	○	○	○	○	26	○	○	○	○	○
7	○	○	○	○	○	27	○	○	○	○	○
8	○	○	○	○	○	28	○	○	○	○	○
9	○	○	○	○	○	29	○	○	○	○	○
10	○	○	○	○	○	30	○	○	○	○	○
11	○	○	○	○	○	31	○	○	○	○	○
12	○	○	○	○	○	32	○	○	○	○	○
13	○	○	○	○	○	33	○	○	○	○	○
14	○	○	○	○	○	34	○	○	○	○	○
15	○	○	○	○	○	35	○	○	○	○	○
16	○	○	○	○	○						
17	○	○	○	○	○						
18	○	○	○	○	○						
19	○	○	○	○	○						
20	○	○	○	○	○						

Practice Test Questions Set 1

Mathematics

	A	B	C	D	E		A	B	C	D	E
1	○	○	○	○	○	21	○	○	○	○	○
2	○	○	○	○	○	22	○	○	○	○	○
3	○	○	○	○	○	23	○	○	○	○	○
4	○	○	○	○	○	24	○	○	○	○	○
5	○	○	○	○	○	25	○	○	○	○	○
6	○	○	○	○	○	26	○	○	○	○	○
7	○	○	○	○	○	27	○	○	○	○	○
8	○	○	○	○	○	28	○	○	○	○	○
9	○	○	○	○	○	29	○	○	○	○	○
10	○	○	○	○	○	30	○	○	○	○	○
11	○	○	○	○	○	31	○	○	○	○	○
12	○	○	○	○	○	32	○	○	○	○	○
13	○	○	○	○	○	33	○	○	○	○	○
14	○	○	○	○	○	34	○	○	○	○	○
15	○	○	○	○	○	35	○	○	○	○	○
16	○	○	○	○	○	36	○	○	○	○	○
17	○	○	○	○	○	37	○	○	○	○	○
18	○	○	○	○	○	38	○	○	○	○	○
19	○	○	○	○	○	39	○	○	○	○	○
20	○	○	○	○	○	40	○	○	○	○	○

Section I – Sequences

1. Consider the following sequence: 1132, 1121, ..., 1199, ... What number comes next?

    a. 1109
    b. 1188
    c. 1189
    d. 1180

2. Consider the following sequence: 64, 50, 38, 28, 20, ... Find the first three terms.

    a. 15, 10, 5
    b. 14, 10, 8
    c. 10, 0, -10
    d. 12, 4, -6

3. 2 4 8 16 | 5 10 20 40 | 4 8 16 32 | 3 6 ... 24

    a. 4
    b. 12
    c. 8
    d. 10

4. Consider the following sequence: 23, ..., 31, 37. What is the missing number?

    a. 19
    b. 27
    c. 29
    d. 30

Practice Test Questions Set 1

5. Consider the following sequence: 3, 6, 11, 18, ...
What number should come next?

    a. 30
    b. 27
    c. 22
    d. 29

6. Consider the following sequence: 26, 24, 20, 14, ...
What number should come next?

    a. 6
    b. 18
    c. 12
    d. 8

7. Consider the following sequence: 6, 8, 4, 10, 18, 22, ... What number should come next?

    a. 34
    b. 32
    c. 24
    d. 26

8. Consider the following sequence: 10, 13, 16, 19, ...
What 3 numbers should come next?

    a. 21, 23, 25
    b. 21, 24, 27
    c. 22, 25, 28
    d. 23, 26, 29

9. Consider the following sequence: 17, 23, 29, 35, ...
What 3 numbers should come next?

    a. 41, 47, 54
    b. 42, 47, 53
    c. 40, 45, 50
    d. 41, 47, 53

10. Consider Box A and the relationship to the numbers in Box B. What is the missing number in Box B?

Box A

8	12
5	9

Box B

19	27
13	?

    a. 18
    b. 21
    c. 24
    d. 14

11. Consider the following sequence:
8, 11, 9, 12, 10, 13, ... What number should come next?

    a. 11
    b. 10
    c. 15
    d. 16

12. Consider the following sequence:
2, 1, (1/2), (1/4), ... What number should come next?

    a. 1/3
    b. 1/8
    c. 1/16
    d. 2/8

Practice Test Questions Set 1

13. Consider the following sequence: 10, 20, 40, 80, ... What number should come next?

   a. 150
   b. 120
   c. 90
   d. 160

14. Consider the following sequence: 18395, 18295, 18195, 18095, ... What number should come next?

   a. 18000
   b. 18950
   c. 17995
   d. 17905

15. Consider the following sequence: -45, -39, -33, -27, ... What number should come next?

   a. 21
   b. -21
   c. -25
   d. 25

16. Consider the following sequence: -100, 100, -200, 0, -300 ... What number should come next?

   a. 0
   b. -200
   c. -100
   d. 100

17. Consider the following sequence:
2.3, 2.3, 4.6, 12.18 ... What number should come next?

    a. 24.36
    b. 48.72
    c. 48
    d. 12.19

18. Consider the following sequence:
3, 9, 11, 33, 36, ... What number should come next?

    a. 106
    b. 39
    c. 33
    d. 108

19. Consider the following sequence:
345, 347, 344, 346, ... What number should come next?

    a. 345
    b. 343
    c. 348
    d. 349

20. Consider the following sequence:
21, 21, 31, 31, 41, 41, ... What number should come next?

    a. 51
    b. 50
    c. 61
    d. 31

Analogies

Choose the pair, or option to complete the pair, that are related in the same way as the given pair.

1. Medicine : Illness

    a. Law : Anarchy

    b. Hunger : Thirst

    c. Etiquette : Discipline

    d. Stimulant : Sensitivity

2. Gold : Metal

    a. Carnivorous : Veterinarian

    b. Surgeon : Doctor

    c. Secretary : Lawyer

    d. Potato : Farmer

3. Melt : Liquid :: Freeze : _____

    a. Ice

    b. Condense

    c. Solid

    d. Steam

4. Clock : Time :: Thermometer : _____

    a. Heat

    b. Radiation

    c. Energy

    d. Temperature

Pass the COOP!

5. Car : Garage :: Plane : _____

    a. Depot
    b. Port
    c. Hanger
    d. Harbor

6. Acting : Theater :: Gambling : _____

    a. Gym
    b. Bar
    c. Club
    d. Casino

7. Pork : Pig :: Beef : _____

    a. Herd
    b. Farmer
    c. Cow
    d. Lamb

8. Fruit : Banana :: Mammal : _____

    a. Cow
    b. Snake
    c. Fish
    d. Sparrow

9. Zoology : Animals

    a. Ecology : Pollution
    b. Botany : Plants
    c. Chemistry : Atoms
    d. History : People

10. Slumber : Sleep :: Bog : _____

    a. Dream
    b. Foray
    c. Swamp
    d. Night

Practice Test Questions Set 1

Choose the word or concept with the closest meaning.

11. Competition

    a. Struggle
    b. Team
    c. Prize
    d. Test

12. Exchange

    a. Gift
    b. Reciprocation
    c. Business
    d. Transfer

13. Insurance

    a. Provision
    b. Indemnity
    c. Occurrence
    d. Accountable

14. History

    a. Experience
    b. Cause
    c. System
    d. Chronological

15. System

    a. Organization
    b. Collection
    c. Relationship
    d. Exhibit

16. Parallel

    a. Skew
    b. Equal
    c. Planes
    d. Intersection

17. Probable

    a. Possibility
    b. Occurrence
    c. Likely
    d. Presumption

18. Opinion

    a. Certainty
    b. Conclusion
    c. Belief
    d. Proof

19. Decision

    a. Outcome
    b. Conclusion
    c. Score
    d. Game

20. Control

    a. Direct
    b. Manage
    c. Adjust
    d. Mechanism

Practice Test Questions Set 1

Quantitative & Verbal Reasoning

Identify the shaded portion of the figures below.

1.

   a. 1/8
   b. 1/4
   c. 1/2
   d. 1/3

2.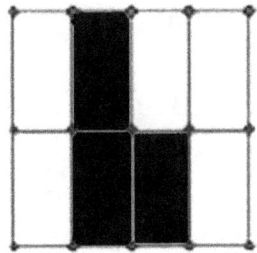

   a. 1/4
   b. 2/8
   c. 3/8
   d. 3/6

3.

a. 1/8

b. 1/4

c. 1/2

d. 1/3

4.

a. 4/9
b. 3/8
c. 1/2
d. 2/3

Practice Test Questions Set 1

5.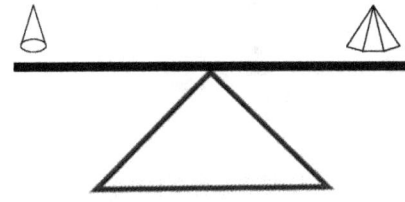

a.   △ △   △ △
b.   △   △ △
c.   △ △ △ △ △
d.   △ △ △ △ △

6.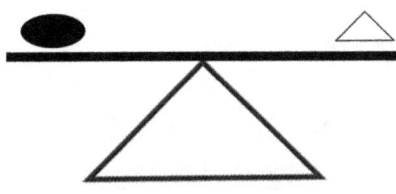

a.   △ △ △   ● ●
b.   ● ●   △
c.   ● ●   △ ●
d.   ●   ● ●

7.

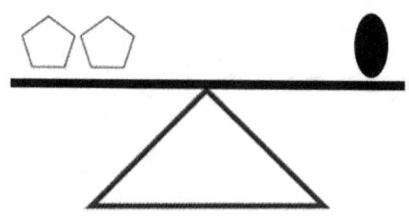

a. ●●⬠   ●⬠⬠⬠
b. ●   ⬠
c. ⬠⬠   ●●⬠
d. ●⬠   ⬠⬠⬠

8.

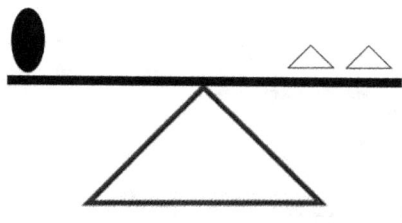

a. ●△   ●●
b. △   ●●
c. ●●   ●△△△
d. ●●   △△△△

Practice Test Questions Set 1   *197*

9.

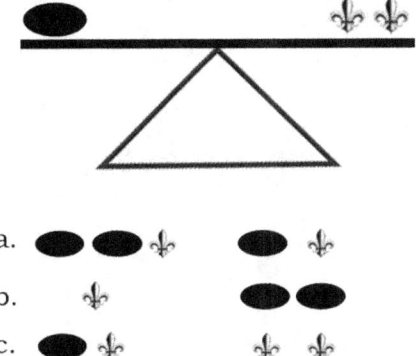

a.
b.
c.
d.

Directions: Consider the relationship between the numbers in column 1 and column 2, then find the missing number.

10.

2 -> 4
3 -> 9
10 -> 100
12 -> ?

    a. 120

    b. 144

    c. 100

    d. 88

11.

1245 -> 1256
1375 -> 1286
4576 -> 4587
1973 -> ?

    a. 1983

    b. 1984

    c. 1987

    d. 1973

12.

2   -> 1
1/2 -> 1/4
12 -> 6
74 -> ?

    a. 25
    b. 37
    c. 52
    d. 19

13.

17 -> 22
22 -> 28
28 -> 35
35 -> ?

    a. 43

    b. 40

    c. 41

    d. 42

Practice Test Questions Set 1

14.

-300 -> 100
-200 -> 200
-700 -> -300
-120 -> ?

    a. 130
    b. 280
    c. -280
    d. 400

15.

47 -> 40
40 -> 34
32 -> 27
25 -> ?

    a. 21
    b. 22
    c. 23
    d. 24

16. Which of the following does not belong?

    a. 121212
    b. 141414
    c. 151415
    d. 292929

17. Which of the following does not belong?

    a. 246
    b. 123
    c. 468
    d. 024

18. Which of the following does not belong?

    a. QRS
    b. LMN
    c. ACF
    d. RST

19. Which of the following does not belong?

    a. aBCd
    b. lMNo
    c. PQRs
    d. tUVw

20. Which of the following does not belong?

    a. ABCD
    b. JKLM
    c. PQRS
    d. WXYZ

21. Which of the following does not belong?

    a. BBCCDDEE
    b. LLMMNNOO
    c. HHIIJJKK
    d. RRSSTTUU

Practice Test Questions Set 1

22. Which of the following does not belong?

   a. 123

   b. 246

   c. 456

   d. 789

23. Which of the following does not belong?

   a. def

   b. nop

   c. tuv

   d. lmn

24. Which of the following does not belong?

   a. Argue

   b. Talk

   c. Dispute

   d. Contest

25. Which of the following does not belong?

   a. ddeeffgg

   b. ffgghhii

   c. nnooppqq

   d. ttuuvvww

26. Which of the following does not belong?

   a. 11223344

   b. 33445566

   c. 33455666

   d. 44556677

27. Big bigger biggest   Small smaller ____

    a. Tiny

    b. Large

    c. Medium

    d. Smallest

28. Thin thinner thinnest   Fat fatter ____

    a. Fattest

    b. Mediocre

    c. Chubby

    d. Medium

29. Sweet sweeter sweetest   Sour more sour ____

    a. Sourest

    b. Most sour

    c. Bitter

    d. Most bitter

30. Young younger youngest   Old older ____

    a. New

    b. Aged

    c. Oldest

    d. Eldest

31. Tom and Tim are brothers. They look exactly the same. They also have the same birthdays.

    a. Tom is older than Tim

    b. Tim is more handsome than Tom

    c. Tom and Tim are twins

    d. Tom and Tim are best friends

Practice Test Questions Set 1

32. Girls love roses. They smell so sweet. Their colors are also very attractive.

    a. Roses are fragrant

    b. Roses attract bees

    c. Boys love roses

    d. Girls don't like roses

33. Rhea helps mother with the household chores everyday. She sweeps the floor every morning. She also helps mother prepare food for the family. She washes the dishes too.

    a. Rhea is helpful.

    b. Rhea is too lazy to do household chores.

    c. Rhea waters the plants.

    d. Rhea cooks for the whole family.

34. John is fond of the color green. He always wears green shirts to school. His rubber shoes are also green. His bag, raincoat, and notebooks are also green.

    a. John has green eyes

    b. John hates the color green

    c. John like the color green

    d. John wears blue rubber shoes to school

35. The Earth is the only planet with known life forms. It is the third planet from the sun in the solar system. It rotates on its axis in 24 hours and revolves around the sun in 365 ¼ days.

    a. There is no life on Earth

    b. The Earth is round

    c. The Earth is the farthest planet in the solar system

    d. Many living things live on Earth

36. Whenever I swim in the ocean I get cold. I went swimming today. I will be getting cold very soon. If the first 2 statements are true, then the third statement is:

    a. True

    b. False

    c. Uncertain

37. Fish can't breathe out of the water. Fish use their gills to breathe. Gills don't work out of water. If the first 2 statements are true, then the third statement is:

    a. True

    b. False

    c. Uncertain

38. I eat steak when I am hungry. I ate steak last night. I was hungry last night. If the first 2 statements are true, then the third statement is:

    a. True

    b. False

    c. Uncertain

39. I read a lot. My favorite author is Herman Melville. I have read all of Herman Melville's books. If the first 2 statements are true, then the third statement is:

    a. True

    b. False

    c. Uncertain

Practice Test Questions Set 1

40. All books are very informative. I am reading a book. I will learn something from this book. If the first 2 statements are true, then the third statement is:

    a. True

    b. False

    c. Uncertain

Part II – Reading and Language Arts

Directions: The following questions are based on several reading passages. A series of questions follow each passage. Read each passage carefully, and then answer the questions based on it. You may reread the passage as often as you wish. When you have finished answering the questions based on one passage, go right onto the next passage. Choose the best answer based on the information given and implied.

Questions 1 – 4 refer to the following passage.

Passage 1 - The Life of Helen Keller

Many people have heard of Helen Keller. She is famous because she was unable to see or hear, but learned to speak and read and went onto attend college and earn a degree. Her life is a very interesting story, one that she developed into an autobiography, which was then adapted into both a stage play and a movie. How did Helen Keller overcome her disabilities to become a famous woman? Read on to find out.
Helen Keller was not born blind and deaf. When she was a small baby, she had a very high fever for several days. As a result of her sudden illness, baby Helen lost her eyesight and her hearing. Because she was so young when she went deaf and blind, Helen Keller never had any recollection of being able to see or hear. Since she could not hear, she could not learn to talk. Since she could not see, it was dif-

ficult for her to move around. For the first six years of her life, her world was very still and dark.

Imagine what Helen's childhood was like. She could not hear her mother's voice. She could not see the beauty of her parent's farm. She could not recognize who was giving her a hug, or a bath or even where her bedroom was each night. Worse, she could not communicate with her parents in any way. She could not express her feelings or tell them the things she wanted. It must have been a very sad childhood.

When Helen was six years old, her parents hired her a teacher named Anne Sullivan. Anne was a young woman who was almost blind. However, she could hear and she could read Braille, so she was a perfect teacher for young Helen. At first, Anne had a very hard time teaching Helen anything. She described her first impression of Helen as a "wild thing, not a child." Helen did not like Anne at first either. She bit and hit Anne when Anne tried to teach her. However, the two of them eventually came to have a great deal of love and respect.

Anne taught Helen to hear by putting her hands on people's throats. She could feel the sounds people made. In time, Helen learned to feel what people said. Next, Anne taught Helen to read Braille, which is a way that books are written for the blind. Finally, Anne taught Helen to talk. Although Helen did learn to talk, it was hard for anyone but Anne to understand her.

As Helen grew older, she amazed more and more people with her story. She went to college and wrote books about her life. She gave talks to the public, with Anne at her side, translating her words. Today, both Anne Sullivan and Helen Keller are famous women who are respected for their lives' work.

Practice Test Questions Set 1

1. Helen Keller could not see and hear and so, what was her biggest problem in childhood?

    a. Inability to communicate

    b. Inability to walk

    c. Inability to play

    d. Inability to eat

2. Helen learned to hear by feeling the vibrations people made when they spoke. What were these vibrations were felt through?

    a. Mouth

    b. Throat

    c. Ears

    d. Lips

3. From the passage, we can infer that Anne Sullivan was a patient teacher. We can infer this because

    a. Helen hit and bit her and Anne remained her teacher.

    b. Anne taught Helen to read only.

    c. Anne was hard of hearing too.

    d. Anne wanted to be a teacher.

4. Helen Keller learned to speak but Anne translated her words when she spoke in public. The reason Helen needed a translator was because

    a. Helen spoke another language.

    b. Helen's words were hard for people to understand.

    c. Helen spoke very quietly.

    d. Helen did not speak but only used sign language.

Questions 5 – 7 refer to the following passage.

Passage 2 - Ways Characters Communicate in Theater

Playwrights give their characters voices in a way that gives depth and added meaning to what happens on stage during their play. There are different types of speech in scripts that allow characters to talk with themselves, with other characters, and even with the audience.

It is very unique to theater that characters may talk "to themselves." When characters do this, the speech they give is called a soliloquy. Soliloquies are usually poetic, introspective, moving, and can tell audience members about the feelings, motivations, or suspicions of an individual character without that character having to reveal them to other characters on stage. "To be or not to be" is a famous soliloquy given by Hamlet as he considers difficult but important themes, such as life and death.

The most common type of communication in plays is when one character is speaking to another or a group of other characters. This is generally called dialogue, but can also be called monologue if one character speaks without being interrupted for a long time. It is not necessarily the most important type of communication, but it is the most common because the plot of the play cannot really progress without it.

Lastly, and most unique to theater (although it has been used somewhat in film) is when a character speaks directly to the audience. This is called an aside, and scripts usually specifically direct actors to do this. Asides are usually comical, an inside joke between the character and the audience, and very short. The actor will usually face the audience when delivering them, even if it's for a moment, so the audience can recognize this move as an aside.

All three of these types of communication are important to the art of theater, and have been perfected by famous playwrights like Shakespeare. Understanding these types of communication can help an audience member grasp what

Practice Test Questions Set 1

is artful about the script and action of a play.

5. According to the passage, characters in plays communicate to

    a. move the plot forward

    b. show the private thoughts and feelings of one character

    c. make the audience laugh

    d. add beauty and artistry to the play

6. When Hamlet delivers "To be or not to be," he can most likely be described as

    a. solitary

    b. thoughtful

    c. dramatic

    d. hopeless

7. The author uses parentheses to punctuate "although it has been used somewhat in film,"

    a. to show that films are less important

    b. instead of using commas so that the sentence is not interrupted

    c. because parenthesis help separate details that are not as important

    d. to show that films are not as artistic

Questions 8 – 11 refer to the following passage.

Passage 3 - Low Blood Sugar

As the name suggest, low blood sugar is low sugar levels in the bloodstream. This can occur when you have not eaten properly and undertake strenuous activity, or, when you are very hungry. When Low blood sugar occurs regularly and is ongoing, it is a medical condition called hypoglycemia. This condition can occur in diabetics and in healthy adults.

Causes of low blood sugar can include excessive alcohol consumption, metabolic problems, stomach surgery, pancreas, liver or kidneys problems, as well as a side-effect of some medications.

Symptoms

There are different symptoms depending on the severity of the case.

Mild hypoglycemia can lead to feelings of nausea and hunger. The patient may also feel nervous, jittery and have fast heart beats. Sweaty skin, clammy and cold skin are likely symptoms.
Moderate hypoglycemia can result in a short temper, confusion, nervousness, fear and blurring of vision. The patient may feel weak and unsteady.

Severe cases of hypoglycemia can lead to seizures, coma, fainting spells, nightmares, headaches, excessive sweats and severe tiredness.

Diagnosis of low blood sugar

A doctor can diagnosis this medical condition by asking the patient questions and testing blood and urine samples. Home testing kits are available for patients to monitor blood sugar levels. It is important to see a qualified doctor though. The doctor can administer tests to ensure that will safely rule out other medical conditions that could affect blood sugar levels.

Treatment

Quick treatments include drinking or eating foods and drinks with high sugar contents. Good examples include soda, fruit juice, hard candy and raisins. Glucose energy tablets can also help. Doctors may also recommend medications and well as changes in diet and exercise routine to treat chronic low blood sugar.

Practice Test Questions Set 1

8. Based on the article, which of the following is true?

    a. Low blood sugar can happen to anyone.

    b. Low blood sugar only happens to diabetics.

    c. Low blood sugar can occur even.

    d. None of the statements are true.

9. Which of the following are the author's opinion?

    a. Quick treatments include drinking or eating foods and drinks with high sugar contents.

    b. None of the statements are opinions.

    c. This condition can occur in diabetics and also in healthy adults.

    d. There are different symptoms depending on the severity of the case

10. What is the author's purpose?

    a. To inform

    b. To persuade

    c. To entertain

    d. To analyze

11. Which of the following is not a detail?

    a. A doctor can diagnosis this medical condition by asking the patient questions and testing.

    b. A doctor will test blood and urine samples.

    c. Glucose energy tablets can also help.

    d. Home test kits monitor blood sugar levels.

    d. None of the above.

Questions 12 – 15 refer to the following passage.

How To Get A Good Nights Sleep

Sleep is just as essential for healthy living as water, air and food. Sleep allows the body to rest and replenish depleted energy levels. Sometimes we may, for various reasons, have trouble sleeping which has a serious effect on our health. Those who have prolonged sleeping problems are facing a serious medical condition and should see a qualified doctor when possible for help. Here is simple guide that can help you sleep better at night.

Try to create a natural pattern of waking up and sleeping around the same time every day. This means avoiding going to bed too early and oversleeping past your usual wake up time. Going to bed and getting up at radically different times everyday confuses your body clock. Try to establish a natural rhythm as much as you can.

Exercises and a bit of physical activity can help you sleep better at night. If you are having problem sleeping, try to be as active as you can during the day. If you are tired from physical activity, falling asleep is a natural and easy process
for your body. If you remain inactive during the day, you will find it harder to sleep properly at night. Try walking, jogging, swimming or simple stretches as you get close to your bed time.

Afternoon naps are great to refresh you during the day, but they may also keep you awake at night. If you feel sleepy during the day, get up, take a walk and get busy to keep from sleeping. Stretching is a good way to increase blood flow to the brain and keep you alert so that you don't sleep during the day. This will help you sleep better night.

A warm bath or a glass of milk in the evening can help your body relax and prepare for sleep. A cold bath will wake you up and keep you up for several hours. Also avoid eating too late before bed.

Practice Test Questions Set 1

12. How would you describe this sentence?

    a. A recommendation

    b. An opinion

    c. A fact

    d. A diagnosis

13. Which of the following is an alternative title for this article?

    a. Exercise and a good night's sleep

    b. Benefits of a good night's sleep

    c. Tips for a good night's sleep

    d. Lack of sleep is a serious medical condition

14. Which of the following cannot be inferred from this article?

    a. Biking is helpful for getting a good night's sleep

    b. Mental activity is helpful for getting a good night's sleep

    c. Eating bedtime snacks is not recommended

    d. Getting up at the same time is helpful for a good night's sleep

15. What is a disadvantage of taking naps?

    a. They may keep you awake.

    b. There are no disadvantages

    c. They may help you sleep better

    d. They may affect your diet

Section II – English Grammar

16. The rules of most sports _____ more complicated than we often realize.

    a. are

    b. is

    c. was

    d. has been

17. Neither of the Wright Brothers _____ that they would be successful with their flying machine.

    a. have any doubts

    b. has any doubts

    c. had any doubts

    d. will have any doubts

18. The Titanic _____ mere days into its maiden voyage.

    a. has already sunk

    b. will already sunk

    c. already sank

    d. sank

19. _____ won first place in the Western Division?

   a. Who
   b. Whom
   c. Which
   d. What

20. Choose the sentence with the correct grammar.

   a. Until you take the overdue books to the library, you can't take any new ones home.

   b. Until you take the overdue books to the library, you can't bring any new ones home.

   c. Until you bring the overdue books to the library, you can't take any new ones home.

   d. Until you take the overdue books to the library, you can't take any new ones home.

21. Choose the sentence with the correct grammar.

   a. Newer cars use fewer gasoline and produce fewer emissions.

   b. Newer cars use less gasoline and produce less emissions.

   c. Newer cars use less gasoline and produce fewer emissions.

   d. Newer cars fewer less gasoline and produce less emissions.

22. Choose the sentence with the correct grammar.

a. His doctor suggested that he eat less snacks and do fewer lounging on the couch.

b. His doctor suggested that he eat fewer snacks and do less lounging on the couch.

c. His doctor suggested that he eat less snacks and do less lounging on the couch.

d. His doctor suggested that he eat fewer snacks and do fewer lounging on the couch.

23. Choose the sentence with the correct grammar.

a. However, I believe that he didn't really try that hard.

b. However I believe that he didn't really try that hard.

c. However; I believe that he didn't really try that hard.

d. However: I believe that he didn't really try that hard.

24. Choose the sentence with the correct grammar.

a. There was however, very little difference between the two.

b. There was, however very little difference between the two.

c. There was; however, very little difference between the two.

d. There was, however, very little difference between the two.

Practice Test Questions Set 1

25. Choose the sentence with the correct grammar.

a. Don would never have thought of that book, but you could have reminded him.

b. Don would never of thought of that book, but you could have reminded him.

c. Don would never have thought of that book, but you could of have reminded him.

d. Don would never of thought of that book, but you could of reminded him.

26. Choose the sentence with the correct grammar.

a. The mother would not of punished her daughter if she could have avoided it.

b. The mother would not have punished her daughter if she could of avoided it.

c. The mother would not of punished her daughter if she could of avoided it.

d. The mother would not have punished her daughter if she could have avoided it.

27. Choose the sentence with the correct grammar.

a. There was scarcely no food in the pantry, because nobody ate at home.

b. There was scarcely any food in the pantry, because nobody ate at home.

c. There was scarcely any food in the pantry, because not nobody ate at home.

d. There was scarcely no food in the pantry, because not nobody ate at home.

28. Choose the sentence with the correct grammar.

a. Although you may not see nobody in the dark, it does not mean that nobody is there.

b. Although you may not see anyone in the dark, it does not mean that not nobody is there.

c. Although you may not see anyone in the dark, it does not mean that no one is there.

d. Although you may not see nobody in the dark, it does not mean that not nobody is there.

29. Choose the sentence with the correct grammar.

a. Michael has lived in that house for forty years, while I has owned this one for only six weeks.

b. Michael have lived in that house for forty years, while I have owned this one for only six weeks.

c. Michael have lived in that house for forty years, while I has owned this one for only six weeks.

d. Michael has lived in that house for forty years, while I have owned this one for only six weeks.

Practice Test Questions Set 1

Combine The Separate Sentences Into One Simpler Sentence With The Same Meaning.

30. The doctor was not looking forward to meeting Mrs. Lucas. The doctor would have to tell Mrs. Lucas that she has cancer. The doctor hated giving bad news to patients.

    a. The doctor hated giving bad news, and so he was not looking forward to meeting Mrs. Lucas because he would have to tell her that she has cancer.

    b. The doctor has cancer and was not looking forward to meeting Mrs. Lucas and telling her this bad news.

    c. Before the doctor met Mrs. Lucas, he had to give his the patients the bad news that Mrs. Lucas has cancer.

    d. The doctor was not looking forward to giving the bad news to his patients that he had to tell Mrs. Lucas that his patients have cancer.

31. Mom hates shopping. We were out of bread, milk and eggs. Mom went to the supermarket.

    a. Because we were out of bread, milk and eggs, Mom hated shopping at the supermarket.

    b. Although she hates shopping, Mom went to the supermarket since we were out of bread, milk and eggs.

    c. Although we were out of bread, milk and eggs, Mom still hated shopping at the supermarket and went there anyway.

    d. Because Mom hated shopping at the supermarket, she went to there to buy her bread, milk and eggs.

Select the Best Revision.

32. Those comic books, which was for sale at the magazine shop, are now quite valuable.

    a. Those comics books which were for sale, at the magazine shop are now quite valuable.

    b. Those comic books, which were for sale at the magazine, shop, are now quite valuable.

    c. Those comic books, which were for sale at the magazine shop, are now, quite valuable

    d. Those comic books, which were for sale at the magazine shop, are now quite valuable.

33. If you want to sell your car, it's important being honest with the buyer.

    a. If you want to sell your car, being honest with the buyer is important.

    b. If you want to sell your car, to be honest with the buyer is important.

    c. If you wanting to sell your car, being honest with the buyer are important.

    d. If you want to selling your car, to be honest with the buyer is important.

34. In Edgar Allen Poe's _____ Edgar Allen Poe describes a man with a guilty conscience.

    a. short story, "The Tell-Tale Heart,"

    b. short story The Tell-Tale Heart,

    c. short story, The Tell-Tale Heart

    d. short story. "the Tell-Tale Heart,"

Practice Test Questions Set 1

35. Billboards are considered an important part of advertising for big business, _____ by their critics.

    a. but, an eyesore;

    b. but, " an eyesore,"

    c. but an eyesore

    d. but-an eyesore-

Section V – Math

1. Simplify 2 1/3 ÷ 1 2/5

    a. 1 2/5
    b. 1 2/3
    c. 1 1/7
    d. 2 2/5

2. 2/3 x 1 4/7 x 5 1/4

    a. 3 1/4
    b. 5 1/2
    c. 6 2/3
    d. 4 2/5

3. Simplify 4 1/5 ÷ 2 1/3

    a. 1 4/5
    b. 2 1/4
    c. 1 3/7
    d. 2 1/4

4. 10/3 x 2 1/4 x 3 1/5

    a. 1 3/4
    b. 24
    c. 7 2/7
    d. 5 1/5

5. Simplify 3 1/9 ÷ 2 2/3

    a. 2 1/5
    b. 2 3/4
    c. 1 1/6
    d. 1 1/4

6. What is -9 + (+6) − (-2)

    a. -3
    b. -1
    c. 5
    d. -5

7. Smith and Simon are playing a card game. Smith will win if a card drawn from a deck of 52 is either a 7 or a diamond, and Simon will win if the drawn card is an even number. Which statement is more likely to be correct?

    a. Simon will win more games.
    b. Smith will win more games.
    c. They have same winning probability.
    d. A decision cannot be made from the provided data.

8. By practicing, a typist increases his typing speed by 2 words per minute daily. If his current typing speed is 18 words per minute and he practice 3 hours a day, then how many hours will he need to practice to attain 40 words per minute?

    a. 27
    b. 30
    c. 33
    d. 36

Practice Test Questions Set 1

9. If the speed of a train is 72 kilometers per hour, what distance will it cover in 12 seconds?

    a. 200 m

    b. 220 m

    c. 240 m

    d. 260 m

10. In a class of 83 students, 72 are present. What percent of the students are absent? Provide answer up to two significant digits.

    a. 12

    b. 13

    c. 14

    d. 15

11. A driver traveled from city A to city B in 1 hour and 13 minutes. On the way, he had to stop at 5 traffic signals, with an average time of 80 seconds. If the distance between the cities is 65 kilometers then what was the average driving speed?

    a. 56.42

    b. 58.77

    c. 60.34

    d. 63.25

12. Mr. Micheal runs a factory. His total assets are $256,800 that consists of a building worth $80,500, machinery worth $125.000 and $51,300 cash. After one year what will be the value of his total assets if he has additional cash of $75,600 and the value of his building has increased by 10% per year, and his machinery depreciated by 20% per year?

    a. $24,3450

    b. $25,2450

    c. $26,4150

    d. $27,2350

13. Martin earns $25,000 as basic pay, $500 rent and $860 for medical insurance. He spends 40% of his total earning on food and clothing, 10% on children's education and pays $800 for utility bills. What percent of his earning he is saving?

    a. 54%

    b. 50%

    c. 47%

    d. 44%

14. Prize money of $1,050 is to be shared among top three contestants in ratio of 7:5:3 as 1st, 2nd and 3rd prizes respectively. How much more money will the 1st prize contestant receive than the 3rd prize contestant?

    a. $210

    b. $280

    c. $350

    d. $490

15. The manager of a weaving factory estimates that if 10 machines run on 100% efficiency for 8 hours, they will produce 1450 meters of cloth. Due to some technical problems, 4 machines run of 95% efficiency and the remaining 6 at 90% efficiency. How many meters of cloth can these machines will produce in 8 hours?

    a. 1479 meters

    b. 1310 meters

    c. 1334 meters

    d. 1285 meters

Practice Test Questions Set 1

16. A car covers a distance in 3.5 hours at an average speed of 60 km/hr. How much time in hours will a motorbike take to cover this distance at an average speed of 40km/hr?

    a. 4.5
    b. 4.75
    c. 5
    d. 5.25

17. A grandfather is 8 times older than his grandson is now. After 6 years, he will be 5 times older than his grandson will. How old is the grandfather now?

    a. 48
    b. 56
    c. 64
    d. 72

18. Solve for n. $5n + (19 - 2)) = 67$.

    a. 21
    b. 10
    c. 15
    d. 7

19. A boy is given 2 apples while his sister is given 8 oranges. What is the ratio between his apples and her oranges?

    a. 1:2
    b. 2:4
    c. 1:4
    d. 2:1

20. A box contains 7 black pencils and 28 blue ones. What is the ratio between the black and blue pens?

    a. 1:4
    b. 2:7
    c. 1:8
    d. 1:9

21. If X + (32 + 356) = 920. What is x?

    a. 450
    b. 388
    c. 532
    d. 623

22. A boy buys 10 candies. The packet contains 3 green candies, 12 red and 9 blue candies. What is the ratio the green, red and blue sweets?

    a. 1:3:4
    b. 1:4:3
    c. 2:3:1
    d. 1:5:4

23. Solve for x. (12 x 12)/x = 12

    a. 12
    b. 13
    c. 8
    d. 14

24. Solve for A. A − (34 x 2) = 18.

    a. 86
    b. 78
    c. 50
    d. 73

25. Solve for X.   X% of 120 = 30.

   a. 15
   b. 12
   c. 4
   d. 25

26. Solve for X. X * 25% of 100 = 76.

   a. 5
   b. 3
   c. 21
   d. 13

27. Solve for X.   X% of 250 = 50.

   a. 30
   b. 35
   c. 25
   d. 20

28. What is the least common multiple of 4 and 3?

   a. 24
   b. 6
   c. 16
   d. 12

29. What is the ratio between 2 gold coins, 6 silver coins and 12 bronze coins?

   a. 2:3:4
   b. 1:2:4
   c. 1:3:6
   d. 2:3:4

30. What is the least common multiple of 8 and 12?

    a. 24
    b. 36
    c. 12
    d. 8

31. Solve for x. -7 + 3x = 20.

    a. 7
    b. 5
    c. 4
    d. 9

32. What is the least common multiple of 2 and 3?

    a. 2
    b. 4
    c. 6
    d. 3

33. Solve for c, when 124 = 12c - 20.

    a. 6
    b. 12
    c. 10
    d. 15

34. Simplify 3 8/9 + 5 5/6.

    a. 8 13/15
    b. 8 3/9
    c. 9 13/18
    d. 8 12/18

Practice Test Questions Set 1

35. Simplify 7 4/5 + 2 2/5.

    a. 5 3/5
    b. 5 1/5
    c. 4 2/5
    d. 5 2/5

36. Translate the following into an equation: three plus a number times 7 equals 42.

    a. 7(3 + X) = 42
    b. 3(X + 7) = 42
    c. 3X + 7 = 42
    d. (3 + 7)X = 42

37. Estimate 5205 / 25

    a. 108
    b. 308
    c. 208
    d. 408

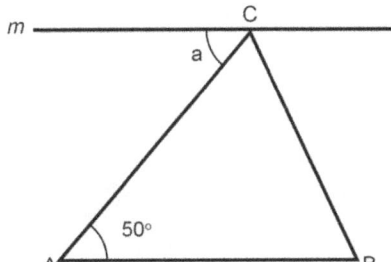

Note: figure not drawn to scale

38. If the line m is parallel to the side AB of △ABC, what is angle a?

    a. 130°
    b. 25°
    c. 65°
    d. 50°

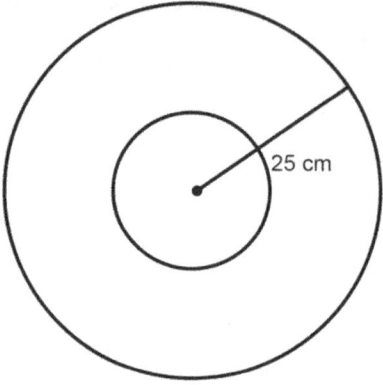

Note: figure not drawn to scale

39. What is the distance traveled by the wheel above, when it makes 175 revolutions?

    a. 87.5 π m
    b. 875 π m
    c. 8.75 π m
    d. 8750 π m

Practice Test Questions Set 1

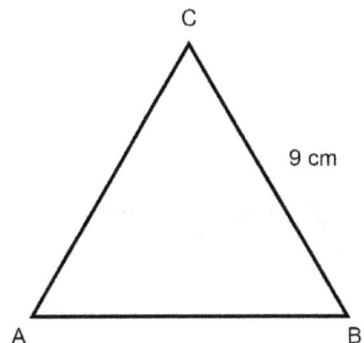

Note: figure not drawn to scale

40. What is the perimeter of the equilateral △ABC above?

    a. 18 cm
    b. 12 cm
    c. 27 cm
    d. 15 cm

Answer Key

Section 1 – Sequences

1. C
Each new element in the sequences includes three instances of the last figure in the previous sequence, plus a new figure.

2. C
The set of figures shifts to the left with each sequence and the set wraps, so the first figure in the first set is the last in the next set.

3. B
Each number in the sequence is double the last number.

4. C
The numbers are consecutive primes (divisible only by 1 and themselves)

5. B
Each number takes the previous number and adds 2.

6. A
Each number decreases by 2, and then increases by the difference between the previous 2 numbers.

7. B
Each number is the sum of the previous and the number 2 places to the left.

8. B
This sequence is increasing by adding 3 to each term.

9. D
Each element in the sequence increases by 6.

10. B
The numbers in Box B are the result of (number in Box A * 2)+ 3. So the missing number is 21.

Practice Test Questions Set 1

11. A
The sequence increases initially and then decreases in the next term. The relationship between each increase is +3 and the relationship with the alternate decrease is -3. So the answer is -2 from the last given term. 13 − 2 = 11.

12. B
The sequence is decreasing by half. So half of 1/4 = 1/8

13. D
The sequence is increasing. Each new term is obtained by multiplying the last term by 2. Therefore, 80 x 2 = 160

14. C
Each new term is calculated by subtracting 100 from the last term. So, 18095 − 100 = 17995

15. B
Each new term is calculated by adding 6 to the last term, therefore, -27 + 6 = -21

16. C
The sequence increases initially and then decreases in the next term. The relationship between each increase is +200 and the relationship with the alternate decrease is -300. So the answer is -300 + 200 = -100

17. B
Each new term is derived by multiplying the last term with an increasing number. The first term is multiplied with 1 to get the next term. That is multiplied with 2 to get the 3rd term, which is multiplied with 3 to get the 4th term. So the answer is 12.18 x 4 = 48.72

18. D
The sequence increases by multiplying by 3 and adding 3. The first term the sequence is increasing by multiplying and adding 3 alternatively. The first term was multiplied by 3 to get the second term, and that was added to 3. The answer = 36 x 3 = 108

19. B
The sequence increases and decreases alternatively. The rate of increase is +2 and decrease is -3, so answer = 346 – 3 = 343

20. A
The sequence is increasing after repeating the last term. The answer = 41 + 10 = 51

Section II - Analogies

1. A
Law cures anarchy in the same way medicine cures illness.

2. B
This is a type relationship. Gold is a type of metal in the same way that a surgeon is a type of doctor.

3. C
This is a process relationship. The first word is the process which creates the second. For example, ice melts to liquid in the same way water freezes to create a solid.

4. D
This is a measurement relationship. Clocks measure time in the same way thermometers measure temperature.

5. C
A car is kept in a garage the same way that a plane is kept in a hangar.

6. D
This is a place relationship. Acting is done in a theater in the same way gambling is done in a casino.

7. C
Pork is the meat of a pig in the same way beef is the meat of a cow.

8. A
This is a classification relationship. The first is the class which the second belongs.

Practice Test Questions Set 1

9. B
The first is the study of the second. Zoology is the study of animals in the same way botany is the study of plants.

10. C
Slumber is a synonym for sleep and bog is a synonym for swamp.

11. D
A competition is a test of skills or abilities between two or more individuals or teams. The winner of a competition is one who can display better abilities in a certain skill or sport.

12. B
An exchange is the reciprocation of gifts, ideas, or other goods; or the act of replacing one thing with another.

13. B
Insurance serves as a means of indemnity or duty owed to an individual as a result of losses or damage.

14. D
History refers to the chronological sequence of events that occur over a given period or time line.

15. A
A system is the organization or way of organizing things amongst its parts or members.

16. B
Parallel refers to things or objects that are of equal distance from one another; such as parallel lines or curves.

17. C
Probable refers to a situation or set of things that cause something to have a high probability in happening based on a set of assumptions or facts.

18. C
An opinion is a set of judgment or beliefs held true which a person is confident and holds true based on facts, moral attitudes, or experience.

19. B

A conclusion is the act of making up one's mind or as a display of firmness of one's character or belief.

20. B

To control something is to manage the limitations through a set of rules or due to one's authority, as well as the use of a controlling device.

Section III - Quantitative & Verbal Reasoning

1. B

1/4 of the figure is shaded.

2. C

3 of the 8 rectangles are shaded representing the fraction 3/8.

3. C

Four of the eight squares are shaded representing the fraction 1/2.

4. A

Four of the nine squares are shaded representing the fraction 4/9.

5. A

The two figures are of equal weight so any combination of equal number.

6. D

The two figures are equal. Choice D is the only combination where the weights are equal.

7. A

Two hexagons equal one oval figure, so cancel out the same and equal figures.

Practice Test Questions Set 1

8. D
One oval figure equals two cones, so choice D, two ovals equal 4 cones.

9. D
One oval figure equals 2 fleur-de-lis, so choice d, 2 ovals equal 4 fleur-de-lis.

10. B
The numbers are squared each time.

11. B
The numbers increase by 11 each time.

12. B
The number decrease by half each time.

13. A
The numbers increase with an increasing amount (1 more each time) starting with 5.

14. C
The number decrease by 400 each time.

15. A
The number decrease by a decreasing amount each time (1 less) starting with 7.

16. C
This is a repetition pattern. All the choices repeat a 2-letter sequence.

17. B
123 are consecutive, the others are obtained by adding 2.

18. C
ACF is not a sequence of consecutive letters.

19. C
Capital small letter relationship. All choices have the middle two letters capitalized except choice c.

20. A
This is a vowel and consonant relationship. All the choices are only consonants.

21. C
This is a vowel and consonant relationship. All the choices have 3 vowels at the end.

22. B
246 is not a sequence of consecutive numbers.

23. D
This is a vowel and consonant relationship. All the choices have one vowel in the middle position.

24. B
This is a word meaning relationship. Talk is not a synonym for any of the choices.

25. B
This is a vowel and consonant relationship. All the choices have vowels in positions 3 and 4.

26. C
This is a repetition pattern. All the choices have consecutive numbers repeated twice.

27. D
All the words are comparative adjectives.

28. A
All the words are comparative adjectives.

29. B
All the words are comparative adjectives.

30. D
All the words are comparative adjectives.

31. C
The only certain thing is they are twins.

Practice Test Questions Set 1

32. A
The only certain thing is roses are fragrant.

33. A
The only certain thing is Rhea is helpful.

34. C
The only certain thing is John likes the color green.

35. D
The only certain thing is many living things live on Earth.

36. C Uncertain.
It does not say where they went swimming.

37. A True.
It must be true that if fish use their gills to breathe, and fish can't breathe out of water, then gills don't work out of water.

38. C Uncertain.
It does not say that they eat steak every time they are hungry.

39. C Uncertain.
It does not say where they went swimming. There could be Herman Melville books they can't find or haven't read.

40. A True.
The answer is true because the first statement says 'all,' Therefore the conclusion is also true. If the first sentence did not say 'all,' the conclusion would not be true.

Section IV – Reading and Language Arts

Part 1 – Reading Comprehension

1. A

The correct answer because that fact is stated directly in the passage. The passage explains that Anne taught Helen to hear by allowing her to feel the vibrations in her throat.

2. B

We can infer that Anne is a patient teacher because she did not leave or lose her temper when Helen bit or hit her; she just kept trying to teach Helen. Choice B is incorrect because Anne taught Helen to read and talk. Choice C is incorrect because Anne could hear. She was partially blind, not deaf. Choice D is incorrect because it does not have to do with patience.

3. A

The passage states that it was hard for anyone but Anne to understand Helen when she spoke. Choice A is incorrect because the passage does not mention Helen spoke a foreign language. Choice C is incorrect because there is no mention of how quiet or loud Helen's voice was. Choice D is incorrect because we know from reading the passage that Helen did learn to speak.

4. B

This question tests the reader's summarization skills. The other choices A, B, and C focus on portions of the second paragraph that are too narrow and do not relate to the specific portion of text in question. The complexity of the sentence may mislead students into selecting one of these answers, but rearranging or restating the sentence will lead the reader to the correct answer. In addition, choice A makes an assumption that may or may not be true about the intentions of the company, choice B focuses on one product rather than the idea of the products, and choice C makes an assumption about women that may or may not be true and is not supported by the text.

Practice Test Questions Set 1

5. D
This question tests the reader's summarization skills. The question is asking very generally about the message of the passage, and the title, "Ways Characters Communicate in Theater," is one indication of that. The other choices A, B, and C are all directly from the text, and therefore readers may be inclined to select one of them, but are too specific to encapsulate the entirety of the passage and its message.

6. B
The paragraph on soliloquies mentions "To be or not to be," and it is from the context of that paragraph that readers may understand that because "To be or not to be" is a soliloquy, Hamlet will be introspective, or thoughtful, while delivering it. It is true that actors deliver soliloquies alone, and may be "solitary" (choice A), but "thoughtful" (choice B) is more true to the overall idea of the paragraph. Readers may choose C because drama and theater can be used interchangeably and the passage mentions that soliloquies are unique to theater (and therefore drama), but this answer is not specific enough to the paragraph in question. Readers may pick up on the theme of life and death and Hamlet's true intentions and select that he is "hopeless" (choice D), but those themes are not discussed either by this paragraph or passage, as a close textual reading and analysis confirms.

7. C
This question tests the reader's grammatical skills. Choice B seems logical, but parenthesis are actually considered to be a stronger break in a sentence than commas are, and along this line of thinking, actually disrupt the sentence more.

Choices A and D make comparisons between theater and film that are simply not made in the passage, and may or may not be true. This detail does clarify the statement that asides are most unique to theater by adding that it is not completely unique to theater, which may have been why the author didn't chose not to delete it and instead used parentheses to designate the detail's importance (choice C).

8. A

Low blood sugar occurs both in diabetics and healthy adults.

9. B

None of the statements are the author's opinion.

10. A

The author's purpose is the inform.

11. A

The only statement that is not a detail is, "A doctor can diagnosis this medical condition by asking the patient questions and testing."

12. A

This sentence is a recommendation.

13. C

Tips for a good night's sleep is the best alternative title for this article.

14. B

Mental activity is helpful for a good night's sleep is cannot be inferred from this article.

15. A

From the passage, one disadvantage of taking naps is they may keep you awake at night.

Part II - English Grammar

16. A

The subject is "rules" so the present tense plural form, "are," is used to agree with "realize."

17. C

The simple past tense, "had," is correct because it refers to completed action in the past.

18. D

The simple past tense, "sank," is correct because it refers to completed action in the past.

Practice Test Questions Set 1

19. A
"Who" is correct because the question uses an active construction. "To whom was first place given?" is passive construction.

20. C
Whether to use "bring" or "take" depends on location. Something coming toward the subject's location is brought. Something going away from the subject's location is taken.

21. C
"Fewer" is used with countable nouns and "less" is used with uncountable nouns.

22. B
"Fewer" is used with countable nouns and "less" is used with uncountable nouns.

23. A
"However" is bracketed with a comma after it at the beginning of a sentence.

24. D
"However" is bracketed with a comma before and after it within a sentence.

25. A
The third conditional is used for talking about an unreal situation (a situation that did not happen) in the past.
For example, "If I had studied harder, [if clause] I would have passed the exam" [main clause]. This has the same meaning as, "I failed the exam, because I didn't study hard enough."

26. D
The third conditional is used for talking about an unreal situation (a situation that did not happen) in the past.
For example, "If I had studied harder, [if clause] I would have passed the exam" [main clause]. This has the same meaning as, "I failed the exam, because I didn't study hard enough."

27. B
In double negative sentences, one negative is replaced with "any."

28. C
In double negative sentences, one negative is replaced with "any."

29. D
The present perfect tense cannot be used with specific time expressions such as yesterday, one year ago, last week, when I was a child, at that moment, that day, one day, etc. The present perfect tense is used with unspecific expressions such as ever, never, once, many times, several times, before, so far, already, yet, etc.

30. A
These three sentences can be combined using 'although,' and 'even if.'

31. B
These two sentences can be combined into one sentence with two clauses separated by a comma.

32. A
The comma separates a phrase starting with 'which.'

33. A
"Being honest," present tense is the best choice. "The buyer" is singular so use "is."

34. A
Titles of short stories are enclosed in quotation marks.

35. C
No additional punctuation is required here.

Section V – Math

1. B
First change all the terms to fractions, therefore, we get

Practice Test Questions Set 1

7/3 / 7/5, to divide we need to invert the second fraction, 7/3 x 5/7, and then we cancel out to reduce to the lowest terms, 1/3 x 5/1 = 5/3, convert back to proper fraction to get 1 2/3

2. B
First, convert all the terms to fractions and then cancel out. Therefore, 2/3 x 11/7 x 21/4 = 2/3 x 11/1 x 3/4, 1/3 x 11/1 x 3/2, 1/1 x 11/1 x 1/2 = 11/2 = 5 1/2

3. A
First change all the terms to fractions, therefore, we get 21/5 / 7/3, to divide we need to invert the second fraction, 21/5 x 3/7, and then we cancel out to reduce to the lowest terms, 3/5 x 3/1 = 9/5, convert back to proper fraction to get 1 4/5

4. B
First, convert all the terms to fractions and then cancel out. Therefore, 10/3 x 9/4 x 16/5 = 10/1 x 3/4 x 16/5, 10/1 x 3/1 x 4/5, 2/1 x 3/1 x 4/1 = 24/1 = 24

5. C
First change all the terms to fractions, 28/9 / 8/3, to divide we need to invert the second fraction, 28/9 x 3/8, and then we cancel out to reduce to the lowest terms, 7/3 x 1/2 = 7/6, convert back to proper fraction to get 1 1/6

6. B
+(+) becomes a positive sign and -(-) equals +, therefore -9 + (+6) − (-2) = -9 + 6 + 2 = -3 + 2 = -1

7. B
There are 52 cards. Smith has 16 cards in which he can win. Therefore, his winning probability in a single game will be 16/52. Simon has 20 cards of wining so his probability of winning in single draw is 20/52. Simon will win more games.

8. C
This is an arithmetic series question where the 1st term is 18 and last term is 40. Expressing the question as a series, we have

18, 20, 22, 24, 26, 28, 30, 32, 34, 36, 38, 40
Therefore, after 11 days of practice he attains that 40 word per minute. As he practices 3 hours daily, the total number of hours required will be 33.

9. C
1 hour is equal to 3600 seconds and 1 kilometer is equal to 1000 meters. Therefore, a train covers 72000 meters in 36000 seconds.
Distance covered in 12 seconds = 12 × 72000/3600 = 240 meters.

10. B
Absent students = 83 − 72 = 11
Percent of absent students =   11/83 X 100 = 13.25
Reducing up to two significant digits will be 13.

Day	Absent	Present	% Attendance
Monday	5	40	88.88%
Tuesday	9	36	80.00%
Wednesday	4	41	91.11%
Thursday	10	35	77.77%
Friday	6	39	86.66%

11. B
Time taken to travel from A to B in seconds = 3600 + (13 X 60) = 3600 + 780 = 4380 seconds.
Total time spent at traffic signals = 80 X 5 = 400 seconds.
The remaining driving time = 4380 − 400 = 3980 seconds = 3980/3600 = 1.106 hours
The speed will be 65/1.106 = 58.77 km/hr

12. C
Cash assets = 75600
Building assets after one year = 80500 X 1.1 = $88550
Machinery assets after one year = 125000 X 0.8 = 100,000
Total value of assets = 264150

13. C
Total earnings = 25000 + 500 + 860 = $26360
Food and Clothing expenses = 0.4 X 26360 = 10544
Children's education expense = 26360 X 0.1 = $2636

Practice Test Questions Set 1   247

Utility Bills = $800
Savings = 26360 − 10544 − 2636 − 800 = $12380
Percent savings = 100 X 12380/26360 = 47%

14. B
1st prize winner receives, 7 X 1050/15 = $490
3rd price winner receives, 3 X 1050/15 = $210
Difference = 490 − 210 = $280

15. C
At 100% efficiency 1 machine produces 1450/10 = 145 m of cloth.

At 95% efficiency, 4 machines produce 4 * 145 * 95/100 = 551 m of cloth.

At 90% efficiency, 6 machines produce 6 * 145 * 90/100 = 783 m of cloth.

Total cloth produced by all 10 machines = 551 + 783 = 1334 m

Since the information provided, and the question, are based on 8 hours, we did not need to use time to reach the answer.

16. D
Distance covered by the car = 60 X 3.5 = 210 km.
Time required by the motorbike = 210/40 = 5.25 hr.

17. C
Let the grandson's age be X and the grandfather's age be Y. According we have,
$y = 8x$
and
$y + 6 = 5(x + 6)$
Solving we get y = 64

18. B
5n + (19 − 2)) = 67, 5n + 17 = 67, 5n = 67 -17, 5n = 50, n = 50/5 = 10

19. C
The ratio between apples and oranges is 2 to 8 or 2:8. Bring to the lowest terms by dividing both sides by 2 gives 1:4.

20. A
The ratio between black and blue pens is 7 to 28 or 7:28. Bring to the lowest terms by dividing both sides by 7 gives 1:4.

21. C
X + 32 + 356 = 920. Therefore X + 388 = 920, X = 920 − 388 = 532

22. B
The ratio between green, red and blue candies is 3:12:9. Bring to the lowest terms by dividing the sides by 3 gives 1:4:3.

23. A
12 x 12 = 144, so 144/x =12, X = 12

24. A
34 x 2 = 68, so A − 68 = 18, A = 68 + 18 = 86

25. D
X% of 120 = 30, so X = 30/120 x 100/1 = 300/12 = 25

This questions can be estimated quickly just by looking at the numbers. 30 and 120 are related by, as 4 X 30 = 120. 4 expressed as a percent is 25%. Check quickly, 25% of 120 = 30.

26. B
X * 25% x 100 = 75, therefore, X * 25 = 75, X = 75/25 = 3

27. D
X% of 250 = 50, so X = 50/250 x 100/1= 100/5 = 20

28. D
Multiples of 3 are 3, 6, 9, 12 and Multiples of 4 are 4, 8, 12, Therefore the least common multiple is 12.

Practice Test Questions Set 1

This can be estimated quickly. 3 is a prime number so the only possible multiples of 3 and any other number, say X, will be 3X.

29. C
The ratio between gold, silver and bronze coins is 2:6:12. Bring to the lowest terms by dividing each element in the original ratio by 2 gives 1:3:6.

30. A
Multiples of 8 are 8, 16, 24 and multiples of 12 are 12, 24, 36, so the least common multiple is 24.

31. D
$3x = 20 + 7 = 27$, $x = 27/3$, $x = 9$.

32. C
Multiples of 2 are 2, 4, 6 and Multiples of 3 are 3, 6, so the least common is 6.

33. B
$124 = 12c - 20$, $124 + 20 = 12c$, $144 = 12c$, $c = 144/12 = 12$.

34. C
Add the whole numbers and then add the fractions, therefore $3 + 5 \{8/9 + 5/6\}$, then find a common denominator for the fractions $8 \{16/18 + 15/18\} = 8\ 31/18$, then simplify to $9\ 13/18$

35. D
Subtract the whole numbers and then subtract the fractions, therefore $7 - 2 \{4/5 - 2/5\}$, the fractions has a common denominator, so
$5 (4-2/5) = 5\ 2/5$.

36. A
Three plus a number times 7 equals 42. Let X be the number.
$(3 + X)$ times $7 = 42$
$7(3 + X) = 42$

37. C
5205 / 25 = 208.20 or, approximately 208.

38. D
Two parallel lines (m & side AB) intersected by side AC
a = 50° (interior angles)

39. A
The wheel travels $2\pi r$ distance when it makes one revolution. Here, r stands for the radius. The radius is given as 25 cm in the figure. So,

$2\pi r = 2\pi * 25 = 50\pi$ cm is the distance traveled in one revolution.

In 175 revolutions: $175 * 50\pi = 8750\pi$ cm is traveled.

We are asked to find the distance in meter.

1 m = 100 cm So;

8750π cm = 8750π / 100 = 87.5π m

40. C
Equilateral triangle with 9 cm sides
Perimeter = 9+9+9
= 27 cm.

Practice Test Questions Set 2

THE PRACTICE TEST PORTION PRESENTS QUESTIONS THAT ARE REPRESENTATIVE OF THE TYPE OF QUESTION YOU SHOULD EXPECT TO FIND ON THE COOP. The questions below are not the same as you will find on the COOP - that would be too easy! And nobody knows what the questions will be and they change all the time. Below are general questions that cover the same areas as the COOP. So, while the format and exact wording of the questions may differ slightly, and change from year to year, if you can answer the questions below, you will have no problem with the COOP.

For the best results, take this Practice Test as if it were the real exam. Set aside time when you will not be disturbed, and a location that is quiet and free of distractions. Read the instructions carefully, read each question carefully, and answer to the best of your ability.

Use the bubble answer sheets provided. When you have completed the Practice Test, check your answer against the Answer Key and read the explanation provided.

Section I – Sequences

Questions: 20

Time: 15 Minutes

Section II – Analogies

Questions: 20

Time: 7 Minutes

Section III – Quantitative and Verbal Reasoning

Questions: 40

Time: 30 Minutes

Section IV – Reading and Language Arts

Questions: 35

Time: 40 Minutes

Section V – Math

Questions: 40

Time: 40 Minutes

Practice Test Questions Set 2

Sequences

	A	B	C	D
1	○	○	○	○
2	○	○	○	○
3	○	○	○	○
4	○	○	○	○
5	○	○	○	○
6	○	○	○	○
7	○	○	○	○
8	○	○	○	○
9	○	○	○	○
10	○	○	○	○
11	○	○	○	○
12	○	○	○	○
13	○	○	○	○
14	○	○	○	○
15	○	○	○	○
16	○	○	○	○
17	○	○	○	○
18	○	○	○	○
19	○	○	○	○
20	○	○	○	○

Analogies

	A	B	C	D
1	○	○	○	○
2	○	○	○	○
3	○	○	○	○
4	○	○	○	○
5	○	○	○	○
6	○	○	○	○
7	○	○	○	○
8	○	○	○	○
9	○	○	○	○
10	○	○	○	○
11	○	○	○	○
12	○	○	○	○
13	○	○	○	○
14	○	○	○	○
15	○	○	○	○
16	○	○	○	○
17	○	○	○	○
18	○	○	○	○
19	○	○	○	○
20	○	○	○	○

Practice Test Questions Set 2

Quantitative & Verbal Reasoning

	A	B	C	D	E			A	B	C	D	E
1	○	○	○	○	○		21	○	○	○	○	○
2	○	○	○	○	○		22	○	○	○	○	○
3	○	○	○	○	○		23	○	○	○	○	○
4	○	○	○	○	○		24	○	○	○	○	○
5	○	○	○	○	○		25	○	○	○	○	○
6	○	○	○	○	○		26	○	○	○	○	○
7	○	○	○	○	○		27	○	○	○	○	○
8	○	○	○	○	○		28	○	○	○	○	○
9	○	○	○	○	○		29	○	○	○	○	○
10	○	○	○	○	○		30	○	○	○	○	○
11	○	○	○	○	○		31	○	○	○	○	○
12	○	○	○	○	○		32	○	○	○	○	○
13	○	○	○	○	○		33	○	○	○	○	○
14	○	○	○	○	○		34	○	○	○	○	○
15	○	○	○	○	○		35	○	○	○	○	○
16	○	○	○	○	○		36	○	○	○	○	○
17	○	○	○	○	○		37	○	○	○	○	○
18	○	○	○	○	○		38	○	○	○	○	○
19	○	○	○	○	○		39	○	○	○	○	○
20	○	○	○	○	○		40	○	○	○	○	○

Reading and Language Arts

	A	B	C	D	E		A	B	C	D	E
1	○	○	○	○	○	21	○	○	○	○	○
2	○	○	○	○	○	22	○	○	○	○	○
3	○	○	○	○	○	23	○	○	○	○	○
4	○	○	○	○	○	24	○	○	○	○	○
5	○	○	○	○	○	25	○	○	○	○	○
6	○	○	○	○	○	26	○	○	○	○	○
7	○	○	○	○	○	27	○	○	○	○	○
8	○	○	○	○	○	28	○	○	○	○	○
9	○	○	○	○	○	29	○	○	○	○	○
10	○	○	○	○	○	30	○	○	○	○	○
11	○	○	○	○	○	31	○	○	○	○	○
12	○	○	○	○	○	32	○	○	○	○	○
13	○	○	○	○	○	33	○	○	○	○	○
14	○	○	○	○	○	34	○	○	○	○	○
15	○	○	○	○	○	35	○	○	○	○	○
16	○	○	○	○	○						
17	○	○	○	○	○						
18	○	○	○	○	○						
19	○	○	○	○	○						
20	○	○	○	○	○						

Practice Test Questions Set 2

Mathematics

	A	B	C	D	E		A	B	C	D	E
1	○	○	○	○	○	21	○	○	○	○	○
2	○	○	○	○	○	22	○	○	○	○	○
3	○	○	○	○	○	23	○	○	○	○	○
4	○	○	○	○	○	24	○	○	○	○	○
5	○	○	○	○	○	25	○	○	○	○	○
6	○	○	○	○	○	26	○	○	○	○	○
7	○	○	○	○	○	27	○	○	○	○	○
8	○	○	○	○	○	28	○	○	○	○	○
9	○	○	○	○	○	29	○	○	○	○	○
10	○	○	○	○	○	30	○	○	○	○	○
11	○	○	○	○	○	31	○	○	○	○	○
12	○	○	○	○	○	32	○	○	○	○	○
13	○	○	○	○	○	33	○	○	○	○	○
14	○	○	○	○	○	34	○	○	○	○	○
15	○	○	○	○	○	35	○	○	○	○	○
16	○	○	○	○	○	36	○	○	○	○	○
17	○	○	○	○	○	37	○	○	○	○	○
18	○	○	○	○	○	38	○	○	○	○	○
19	○	○	○	○	○	39	○	○	○	○	○
20	○	○	○	○	○	40	○	○	○	○	○

Section I – Sequences

1. A D G   J M P   S V Y _____

    a. B N P
    b. O L M
    c. M P S
    d. B E F

2. ααβΩΩμ   ββΩμμα   Ω_____

    a. αβΩμα
    b. μΩΩαβ
    c. Ωμααβ
    d. Ωββαμ

3. Consider the following sequence: 11, 15, 20, 26, ... What 3 numbers should come next?

    a. 31, 37, 42
    b. 33, 41, 50
    c. 32, 38, 46
    d. 36, 46, 56

4. αβαβμ   ΩπΩπ$ β∞β∞©   ¥_____

    a. π¥μ β
    b. μπ¥α
    c. π¥πα
    d. ¥β∞Ω

Practice Test Questions Set 2

5. +-++-+   *÷**÷*   ×=××=

    _____

   a. &*+#=×
   b. +==÷&&
   c. #!%#!$
   d. !#!!#!

6. S S S SS   S S SS SS   S SS SS SS

   _____

   a. S SS SSS SSS
   b. SS SS SS SS
   c. S SS SSS SSSS
   d. S SS SS S

7. Consider the following sequence: 1000, 992, 984, 976, ... What 2 numbers should come next?

   a. 968, 961
   b. 967, 960
   c. 968, 960
   d. 970, 964

8. Consider the following sequence: 0.1, 0.3, 0.9, 2.7, ... What 2 numbers should come next?

   a. -8.1, -24.3
   b. 8.1, 24.3
   c. 5.4, 10.8
   d. -5.4, -10.8

9. Consider the following sequence: 32, 16, 8, 4, ...
What 3 numbers should come next?

   a. 2, 1, 0.5
   b. 2, 0, -2
   c. 0, -4, -8
   d. 2, 1, 0

10. Consider the following sequence: 3, ..., 9, 12, 15.
What is the missing number?

   a. 4
   b. 7
   c. 6
   d. 5

11. Consider the following sequence: 13, ..., 31, 0, 49, 58. What 2 numbers are missing?

   a. 19, 29
   b. 23, 41
   c. 22, 40
   d. 16, 24

12. Consider the following sequence: 95, 90, ..., 80, 75.
What is the missing number?

   a. 87
   b. 85
   c. 86
   d. 80

Practice Test Questions Set 2

13. Consider the following sequence: ..., 75, 65, 70, 60, 65, 55, ... What 2 numbers are missing?

    a. 70, 35
    b. 65, 35
    c. 70, 60
    d. 65, 30

14. Consider the following sequence: 91, 85, ..., ..., 67, 61. What 2 numbers are missing?

    a. 81, 71
    b. 78, 72
    c. 80, 70
    d. 79, 73

15. Consider the following sequence: ..., ..., 120, 129, 138, 147. Find the first two terms.

    a. 102, 111
    b. 100, 110
    c. 102, 112
    d. 99, 111

16. Consider the following sequence: ..., 95, 88, 93, 86, 91, 0. What 2 numbers are missing?

    a. 88, 98
    b. 90, 98
    c. 100, 84
    d. 90, 84

17. Consider the following sequence: 76, 64, 54, 46, ..., 36, 34, ... What 2 numbers are missing?

   a. 40, 32
   b. 40, 34
   c. 42, 30
   d. 42, 32

18. Consider the following sequence: 3, 0, 12, 0, 48, 96. What 2 numbers are missing?

   a. 6, 36
   b. 6, 18
   c. 8, 16
   d. 6, 24

19. Consider the following sequence: 13, ..., 31, 0, 49, 58. What 2 numbers are missing?

   a. 19, 29
   b. 23, 41
   c. 22, 40
   d. 16, 24

20. Consider the following sequence: 3, 13, 22, 30, 37, ... What number comes next?

   a. 45
   b. 47
   c. 43
   d. 42

Practice Test Questions Set 2

Section II – Analogies

Select the word or pair that has the same relationship.

1. Child : Human

    a. Dog : Pet
    b. Kitten : Cat
    c. Cow : Milk
    d. Bird : Robin

2. Wax : Candle

    a. Ink : Pen
    b. Clay : Bowl
    c. String : Kite
    d. Liquid : Cup

3. Petal : Flower :: Fur : ____

    a. Coat
    b. Warm
    c. Woman
    d. Rabbit

4. Present : Birthday :: Reward : _____

    a. Accomplishment
    b. Medal
    c. Acceptance
    d. Cash

5. Shovel : Dig :: Scissors : _____

   a. Scoop
   b. Carry
   c. Snip
   d. Rip

6. Finger : Hand :: Leg : _____

   a. Body
   b. Foot
   c. Toe
   d. Hip

7. Sleep in : Late :: Skip Breakfast : _____

   a. Hungry
   b. Early
   c. Lunch
   d. dinner

8. Circle : Sphere :: Square : _____

   a. Triangle
   b. Oval
   c. Half Circle
   d. Cube

9. Orange : Fruit :: Carrot: _____

   a. Vegetable
   b. Bean
   c. Food
   d. Apple

10. Paper : Light :: Lead : _____

    a. Grey

    b. Solid

    c. Thick

    d. Heavy

11. Steel : Car :: Glass : _____

    a. Pane

    b. Window

    c. Transparent

    d. Fragile

Choose the word that expresses the same concept or quality as the given word.

12. Quality

    a. Excellence

    b. Defect

    c. Measure

    d. Consistency

13. Fiction

    a. Invention

    b. Fact

    c. Molding

    d. Imagination

14. Desire

    a. Attraction

    b. Connection

    c. Longing

    d. Need

15. Responsible

    a. Office
    b. Management
    c. Control
    d. Accountability

16. Tendency

    a. Proneness
    b. Occurrence
    c. Trend
    d. Direction

17. Theory

    a. Explanation
    b. Event
    c. Outcome
    d. Situation

18. Expansion

    a. Growth
    b. Limit
    c. Distance
    d. Circulation

19. Approval

    a. Favorable
    b. Proposal
    c. Expression
    d. Result

Practice Test Questions Set 2

20. Measure
- a. Weight
- b. Size
- c. Scale
- d. Distance

Section III – Quantitative Reasoning

Select the fraction that corresponds to the shaded squares shown.

1.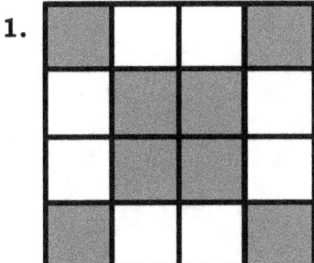

- a. 3/9
- b. 4/9
- c. 1/3
- d. 4/7

2.

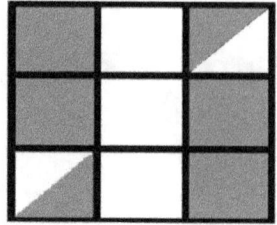

a. 5/9
b. 4/9
c. 1/3
d. 4/7

3.

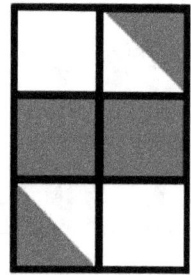

a. 1/2
b. 1/3
c. 2/8
d. 1/5

Practice Test Questions Set 2

4.

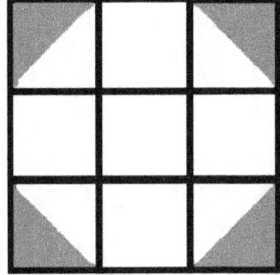

a. 1/3
b. 4/9
c. 2/9
d. 2/6

5.

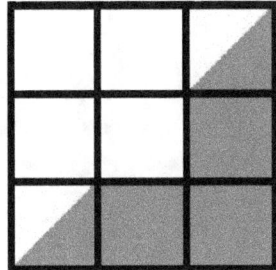

a. 3/9
b. 4/9
c. 4/8
d. 5/9

6.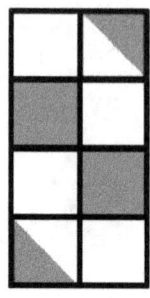

   a. 1/3
   b. 4/6
   c. 4/8
   d. 3/8

7.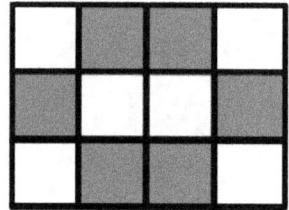

   a. 1/2
   b. 1/3
   c. 6/10
   d. 5/9

8.

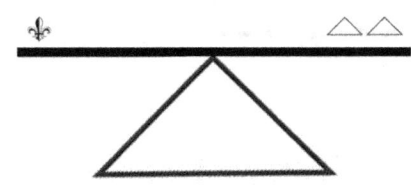

a. △   ⚜
b. ⚜ △△   △△△△
c. △△   ⚜ △
d. ⚜ ⚜   △△△ ⚜

9.

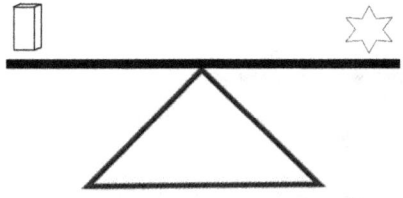

a. ▯ ☆   ☆ ☆ ☆
b. ▯ ▯   ☆
c. ▯ ▯   ☆ ▯
d. ▯ ▯ ▯   ☆ ☆

10.

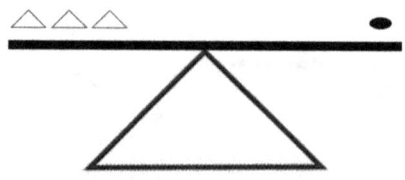

a. △△△ △△△
b. ● △   △△●
c. ● ●   △△●
d. ● △   △△

11.

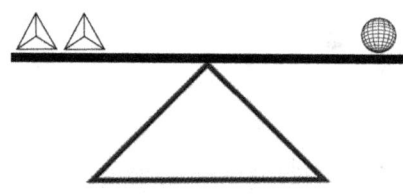

a. △   ● ●
b. ● ●   △ ●
c. △ ●   △△△
d. ● ●   △△△

Practice Test Questions Set 2

12.

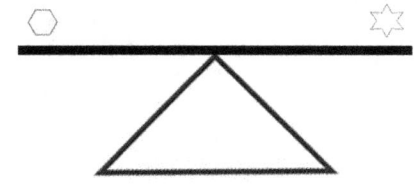

    a. ☆☆   ○○

    b. ☆☆☆   ○☆

    c. ○○   ☆

    d. ☆○   ☆☆

13.

2 -> 5
10 -> 25
30 -> 75
40 -> ?

    a. 100
    b. 80
    c. 120
    d. 75

14.

15 -> 8
-2 -> -8
30 -> 22
-6 -> ?

    a. 13
    b. 1
    c. -13
    d. -5

15.

21 -> 14
45 -> 30
48 -> 36
75 -> ?

    a. 45
    b. 48
    c. 50
    d. 60

16. The children enjoy playing football after school. Sometimes, they play basketball with other kids. On weekends, they play baseball, badminton, or tennis.

    a. Children prefer playing indoors
    b. Children enjoy different kinds of sports
    c. Children hate playing
    d. Playing is a form of exercise

17. All students carry backpacks. My grandfather carries a backpack. Therefore, my grandfather is a student. If the first 2 statements are true, then the third statement is:

    a. True
    b. False
    c. Uncertain

18. Jane spends her free time reading. She likes to read books, magazines, and even newspapers. She reads stories about adventures and fairy tales.

    a. Jane likes to watch television
    b. Jane spends her free time writing stories
    c. Jane's hobby is reading
    d. Jane reads stories in school

Practice Test Questions Set 2

19. The body is made up of many bones. The skull protects the head. The ribs protect the chest. There are also small bones that protect the ears.

    a. Bones are connected to the muscles

    b. Bones are present in the stomach

    c. Animals have bones

    d. Bones protect different parts of the body

20. Doctors can sometimes predict epidemics. Bird Flu is becoming an epidemic. Doctors know where bird flu will spread.

If the first 2 statements are true, then the third statement is:

    a. True

    b. False

    c. Uncertain

21. The silver fish can swim faster than the black fish. The gold fish can swim faster than the black fish. The gold fish can swim faster than the silver fish.

If the first 2 statements are true, then the third statement is:

    a. True

    b. False

    c. Uncertain

22. All dogs are mammals. No cats are dogs. Therefore, no cats are mammals.

If the first 2 statements are true, then the third statement is:

    a. True

    b. False

    c. Uncertain

23. All rabbits have fur. Some rabbits are pets. Some pets have fur.

If the first 2 statements are true, then the third statement is:
   a. True
   b. False
   c. Uncertain

24. All cats are felines. All cats are mammals. All mammals are felines.

If the first 2 statements are true, then the third statement is:

   a. True
   b. False
   c. Uncertain

25. Deciduous trees drop their leaves in the fall. Confers keep their leaves all year round. Conifers are deciduous.

If the first 2 statements are true, then the third statement is:
   a. True
   b. False
   c. Uncertain

Practice Test Questions Set 2

Questions 1 - 4 refer to the following passage.

Passage 1 - The Crusades

In 1095 Pope Urban II proclaimed the First Crusade with the intent and stated goal to restore Christian access to holy places in and around Jerusalem. Over the next 200 years there were 6 major crusades and numerous minor crusades in the fight for control of the "Holy Land." Historians are divided on the real purpose of the Crusades, some believing that it was part of a purely defensive war against Islamic conquest; some see them as part of a long-running conflict at the frontiers of Europe; and others see them as confident, aggressive, papal-led expansion attempts by Western Christendom. The impact of the crusades was profound, and judgment of the Crusaders ranges from laudatory to highly critical. However, all agree that the Crusades and wars waged during those crusades were brutal and often bloody. Several hundred thousand Roman Catholic Christians joined the Crusades, they were Christians from all over Europe.

Europe at the time was under the Feudal System, so while the Crusaders made vows to the Church they also were beholden to their Feudal Lords. This led to the Crusaders not only fighting the Saracen, the commonly used word for Muslim at the time, but also each other for power and economic gain in the Holy Land. This infighting between the Crusaders is why many historians hold the view that the Crusades were simply a front for Europe to invade the Holy Land for economic gain in the name of the Church. Another factor contributing to this theory is that while the army of crusaders marched towards Jerusalem they pillaged the land as they went. The church and feudal Lords vowing to return the land to its original beauty, and inhabitants, this rarely happened though as the Lords often kept the land for themselves. A full 800 years after the Crusades, Pope John Paul II expressed his sorrow for the massacre of innocent people and the lasting damage the Medieval church caused in that area of the World.

Pass the COOP!

1. What is the tone of this article?

    a. Subjective

    b. Objective

    c. Persuasive

    d. None of the Above

2. What can all historians agree on concerning the Crusades?

    a. It achieved great things

    b. It stabilized the Holy Land

    c. It was bloody and brutal

    d. It helped defend Europe from the Byzantine Empire

3. What impact did the feudal system have on the Crusades?

    a. It unified the Crusaders

    b. It helped gather volunteers

    c. It had no effect on the Crusades

    d. It led to infighting, causing more damage than good

4. What does Saracen mean?

    a. Muslim

    b. Christian

    c. Knight

    d. Holy Land

Practice Test Questions Set 2

Questions 5 - 8 refer to the following passage.

ABC Electric Warranty

ABC Electric Company warrants that its products are free from defects in material and workmanship. Subject to the conditions and limitations set forth below, ABC Electric will, at its option, either repair or replace any part of its products that prove defective due to improper workmanship or materials.

This limited warranty does not cover any damage to the product from improper installation, accident, abuse, misuse, natural disaster, insufficient or excessive electrical supply, abnormal mechanical or environmental conditions, or any unauthorized disassembly, repair, or modification.

This limited warranty also does not apply to any product on which the original identification information has been altered, or removed, has not been handled or packaged correctly, or has been sold as second-hand.

This limited warranty covers only repair, replacement, refund or credit for defective ABC Electric products, as provided above.

5. I tried to repair my ABC Electric blender, but could not, so can I get it repaired under this warranty?

    a. Yes, the warranty still covers the blender

    b. No, the warranty does not cover the blender

    c. Uncertain. ABC Electric may or may not cover repairs under this warranty

6. My ABC Electric fan is not working. Will ABC Electric provide a new one or repair this one?

    a. ABC Electric will repair my fan

    b. ABC Electric will replace my fan

    c. ABC Electric could either replace or repair my fan can request either a replacement or a repair.

7. My stove was damaged in a flood. Does this warranty cover my stove?

    a. Yes, it is covered.

    b. No, it is not covered.

    c. It may or may not be covered.

    d. ABC Electric will decide if it is covered

8. Which of the following is an example of improper workmanship?

    a. Missing parts

    b. Defective parts

    c. Scratches on the front

    d. None of the above

Questions 9 – 12 refer to the following passage.

Passage 2 - Women and Advertising

Only in the last few generations have media messages been so widespread and so readily seen, heard, and read by so many people. Advertising is an important part of both selling and buying anything from soap to cereal to jeans. For whatever reason, more consumers are women than are men. Media message are subtle but powerful, and more attention has been paid lately to how these message affect women.
Of all the products that women buy, makeup, clothes, and other stylistic or cosmetic products are among the most popular. This means that companies focus their advertising on women, promising them that their product will make her feel, look, or smell better than the next company's product will. This competition has resulted in advertising that is more and more ideal and less and less possible for everyday women. However, because women do look to these ideals and the products they represent as how they can potentially become, many women have developed unhealthy attitudes about themselves when they have failed

to become those ideals.

In recent years, more companies have tried to change advertisements to be healthier for women. This includes featuring models of more sizes and addressing a huge outcry against unfair tools such as airbrushing and photo editing. There is debate about what the right balance between real and ideal is, because fashion is also considered art and some changes are made to purposefully elevate fashionable products and signify that they are creative, innovative, and the work of individual people. Artists want their freedom protected as much as women do, and advertising agencies are often caught in the middle.

Some claim that the companies who make these changes are not doing enough. Many people worry that there are still not enough models of different sizes and different ethnicities. Some people claim that companies use this healthier type of advertisement not for the good of women, but because they would like to sell products to the women who are looking for these kinds of messages. This is also a hard balance to find: companies do need to make money, and women do need to feel respected.

While the focus of this change has been on women, advertising can also affect men, and this change will hopefully be a lesson on media for all consumers.

9. The second paragraph states that advertising focuses on women

       a. to shape what the ideal should be

       b. because women buy makeup

       c. because women are easily persuaded

       d. because of the types of products that women buy

10. According to the passage, fashion artists and female consumers are at odds because

    a. there is a debate going on and disagreement drives people apart

    b. both of them are trying to protect their freedom to do something

    c. artists want to elevate their products above the reach of women

    d. women are creative, innovative, individual people

11. The author uses the phrase "for whatever reason" in this passage to

    a. keep the focus of the paragraph on media messages and not on the differences between men and women

    b. show that the reason for this is unimportant

    c. argue that it is stupid that more women are consumers than men

    d. show that he or she is tired of talking about why media messages are important

12. This passage suggests that

    a. advertising companies are still working on making their messages better

    b. all advertising companies seek to be more approachable for women

    c. women are only buying from companies that respect them

    d. artists could stop producing fashionable products if they feel bullied

Practice Test Questions Set 2

Questions 13 - 16 refer to the following passage.

FDR, the Treaty of Versailles, and the Fourteen Points

At the conclusion of World War I, those who had won the war and those who were forced to admit defeat welcomed the end of the war and expected that a peace treaty would be signed. The American president, Franklin D. Roosevelt, played an important part in proposing what the agreements should be and did so through his Fourteen Points. World War I had begun in 1914 when an Austrian archduke was assassinated, leading to a domino effect that pulled the world's most powerful countries into war on a large scale. The war catalyzed the creation and use of deadly weapons that had not previously existed, resulting in a great loss of soldiers on both sides of the fighting. More than 9 million soldiers were killed.

The United States agreed to enter the war right before it ended, and many believed that its decision to become finally involved brought on the end of the war. FDR made it very clear that the U.S. was entering the war for moral reasons and had an agenda focused on world peace. The Fourteen Points were individual goals and ideas (focused on peace, free trade, open communication, and self reliance) that FDR wanted the power nations to strive for now that the war had concluded. He was optimistic and had many ideas about what could be accomplished through and during the post-war peace. However, FDR's fourteen points were poorly received when he presented them to the leaders of other world powers, many of whom wanted only to help their own countries and to punish the Germans for fueling the war, and they fell by the wayside. World War II was imminent, for Germany lost everything.

Some historians believe that the other leaders who participated in the Treaty of Versailles weren't receptive to the Fourteen Points because World War I was fought almost entirely on European soil, and the United States lost much less than did the other powers. FDR was in a unique position to determine the fate of the war, but doing it on his own terms did not help accomplish his goals. This is only one historical example of how the United State has tried to use its power as an important country, but found itself limited because of geological or ideological factors.

13. The main idea of this passage is that

    a. World War I was unfair because no fighting took place in America

    b. World War II happened because of the Treaty of Versailles

    c. the power the United States has to help other countries also prevents it from helping other countries

    d. Franklin D. Roosevelt was one of the United States' smartest presidents

14. According to the second paragraph, World War I started because

    a. an archduke was assassinated

    b. weapons that were more deadly had been developed

    c. a domino effect of allies agreeing to help each other

    d. the world's most powerful countries were large

15. The author includes the detail that 9 million soldiers were killed

    a. to demonstrate why European leaders were hesitant to accept peace

    b. to show the reader the dangers of deadly weapons

    c. to make the reader think about which countries lost the most soldiers

    d. to demonstrate why World War II was imminent

Section II – English Grammar

16. There are now several ways to listen to music, including radio, CDs, and Mp3 files _____ you can download onto an MP3 player.

    a. on which
    b. who
    c. whom
    d. which

17. As the tallest monument in the United States, the St. Louis Arch _____.

    a. has rose to an impressive 630 feet.
    b. is risen to an impressive 630 feet.
    c. rises to an impressive 630 feet.
    d. was rose to an impressive 630 feet.

18. The tired, old woman should _____ on the sofa.

    a. lie
    b. lays
    c. laid
    d. lain

19. Did the students understand that Thanksgiving always _____ on the fourth Thursday in November?

    a. fallen
    b. falling
    c. has fell
    d. falls

20. Collecting stamps, _____ and listening to short-wave radio were Rick's main hobbies.

    a. building models,

    b. to build models,

    c. having built models,

    d. build models,

21. This morning, _____ and before the sun came up, my mother makes herself a cup of cocoa.

    a. after the kids had left for school

    b. after the kids leave for school

    c. after the kids have left for school

    d. after the kids will leave for school

22. After the car was fixed, it _____ again.

    a. ran good

    b. ran well

    c. would have run well

    d. ran more well

23. "Where does the sun go during the _____ asked little Kathy.

    a. night,"

    b. night"?,

    c. night,?"

    d. night?"

Practice Test Questions Set 2

24. Choose the sentence with the correct grammar.

a. The older children have already eat their dinner, but the baby has not yet eaten anything.

b. The older children have already eaten their dinner, but the baby has not yet ate anything.

c. The older children have already eaten their dinner, but the baby has not yet eaten anything.

d. The older children have already eat their dinner, but the baby has not yet ate anything.

25. Choose the sentence with the correct grammar.

a. If they had gone to the party, he would have gone, too.

b. If they had went to the party, he would have gone, too.

c. If they had gone to the party, he would have went, too.

d. If they had went to the party, he would have went, too.

26. Choose the sentence with the correct grammar.

a. He should have went to the appointment; instead, he went to the beach.

b. He should have gone to the appointment; instead, he went to the beach.

c. He should have went to the appointment; instead, he gone to the beach.

d. He should have gone to the appointment; instead, he gone to the beach.

27. Choose the sentence with the correct grammar.

a. Lee pronounced it's name incorrectly; it's an impatiens, not an impatience.

b. Lee pronounced its name incorrectly; its an impatiens, not an impatience.

c. Lee pronounced it's name incorrectly; its an impatiens, not an impatience.

d. Lee pronounced its name incorrectly; it's an impatiens, not an impatience.

28. Choose the sentence with the correct grammar.

a. Its important for you to know its official name; its called the Confederate Museum.

b. It's important for you to know it's official name; it's called the Confederate Museum.

c. It's important for you to know its official name; it's called the Confederate Museum.

d. Its important for you to know it's official name; it's called the Confederate Museum.

Select the Best Revision.

29. Although today the boy was nice to my brother, they usually was quite mean to him.

a. Although today the boy was nice to my brother, they were usually quite mean to him.

b. Although today the boy was nice to my brother, he was usually quite mean to him.

c. Although today the boy were nice to my brother, he is usually quite mean to him.

d. Although today the boy was nice to my brother, he were usually quite mean to him.

Practice Test Questions Set 2

Combine The Separate Sentences Into a Simpler Sentence With The Same Meaning.

30. I hate needles. I want to give blood. I can't give blood.

    a. Although I hate needles, I can't give blood even even if I wanted to.

    b. Because I hate needles, I can't give blood, although I want to.

    c. Whenever I hate needles, I give blood although I can't give blood.

    d. Whenever I can't give blood, I give blood anyway, although I hate needles.

31. Choose the sentence with the correct usage.

    a. The principal of the school lived by one principle: always do your best.

    b. The principle of the school lived by one principle: always do your best.

    c. The principal of the school lived by one principal: always do your best.

    d. The principle of the school lived by one principal: always do your best.

32. Choose the sentence with the correct usage.

    a. Even with an speed limit sign clearly posted, an inattentive driver may drive too fast.

    b. Even with a speed limit sign clearly posted, a inattentive driver may drive too fast.

    c. Even with an speed limit sign clearly posted, a inattentive driver may drive too fast.

    d. Even with a speed limit sign clearly posted, an inattentive driver may drive too fast.

33. Choose the sentence with the correct usage.

a. Except for the roses, she did not accept John's frequent gifts.

b. Accept for the roses, she did not except John's frequent gifts.

c. Accept for the roses, she did not accept John's frequent gifts.

d. Except for the roses, she did not except John's frequent gifts.

34. Choose the sentence with the correct usage.

a. Although he continued to advise me, I no longer took his advice.

b. Although he continued to advice me, I no longer took his advise.

c. Although he continued to advise me, I no longer took his advise.

d. Although he continued to advice me, I no longer took his advise.

35. Choose the sentence with the correct usage.

a. To adopt to the climate, we had to adopt a different style of clothing.

b. To adapt to the climate, we had to adapt a different style of clothing.

c. To adapt to the climate, we had to adopt a different style of clothing.

d. To adapt to the climate, we had to adapt a different style of clothing.

Practice Test Questions Set 2

Section IV - Math

1. The sum of the digits of a 2-digit number is 12. If we switch the digits, the number we get will be greater than the initial one by 36. Find the initial number.

    a. 39
    b. 48
    c. 57
    d. 75

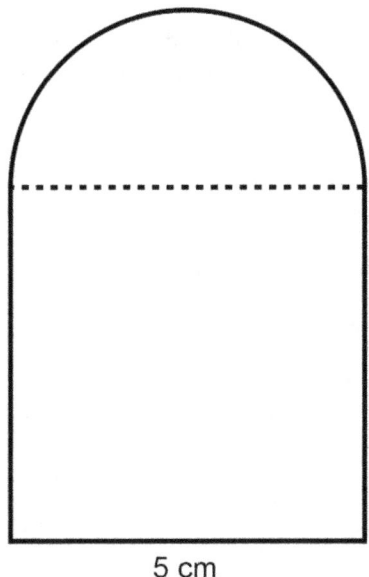

5 cm

Note: figure not drawn to scale

2. What is the perimeter of the above shape, assuming the bottom portion is square?

    a. 17.5 π cm
    b. 20 π cm
    c. 15 π cm
    d. 25 π cm

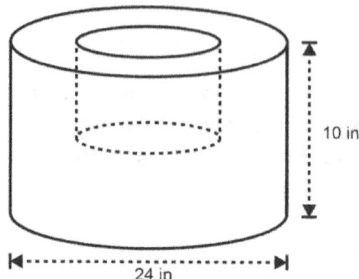

Note: figure not drawn to scale

3. What is the volume of the above solid made by a hollow cylinder that is half the size (in all dimensions) of the larger cylinder?

    a. 1440 π in³
    b. 1260 π in³
    c. 1040 π in³
    d. 960 π in³

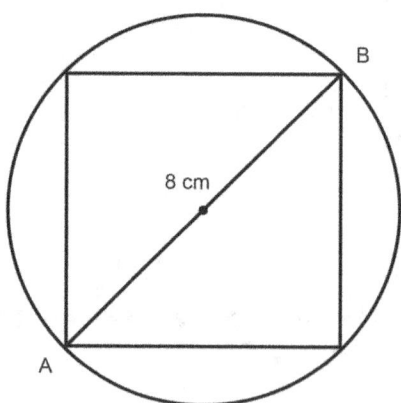

Note: figure not drawn to scale

Practice Test Questions Set 2

4. What is area of the circle?

a. 4 π cm²
b. 12 π cm²
c. 10 π cm²
d. 16 π cm²

5. John jogs around a 75-meter diameter track 7 times. How much linear distance did he cover?

a. 1250 meters
b. 1450 meters
c. 1650 meters
d. 1725 meters

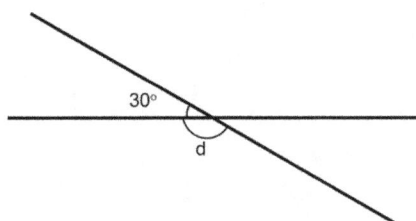

6. What is the indicated angle above?

a. 150°
b. 330°
c. 60°
d. 120°

7. On a circular jogging track with a circumference of 1.2 km, John, Tony and David walk at the rate of 120, 100 and 75 meters per minute respectively. If they all start walking in the same direction, how long will it take until they are together again?

    a. 200 minutes
    b. 220 minutes
    c. 240 minutes
    d. 260 minutes

8. On a scaled map, city A is 12.4 cm away from city B. If the scale is 1 cm = 5 km then what is the actual distance between these two cities?

    a. 12.4 km
    b. 48.4 km
    c. 58 km
    d. 62 km

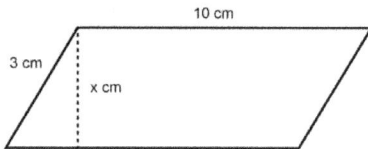

Note: figure not drawn to scale

9. What is the perimeter of the parallelogram above?

    a. 12 cm
    b. 26 cm
    c. 13 cm
    d. (13+x) cm

Practice Test Questions Set 2

10. Estimate 2009 x 108.

    a. 110,000

    b. 2,0000

    c. 21,000

    d. 210,000

11. The playing times for three songs on a compact disc are as follows: 4 minutes 56 seconds for song A, 2 minutes 30 seconds for song B, 10 minutes 16 seconds for song C. What is the average playing time for the three songs?

    a. 17 minutes 42 seconds

    b. 6 minutes 7 seconds

    c. 6 minutes

    d. 5 minutes 54 seconds

12. John is a barber and receives 40% of the amount paid by his customers, and all the tips. If a customer pays $8.50 for a haircut and leaves a tip of $1.30, how much money does John receive?

    a. $3.92

    b. $4.70

    c. $5.30

    d. $6.40

13. The length of a rectangle is 5 in. more than its width. The perimeter of the rectangle is 26 in. What is the width and length of the rectangle?

    a. Width 6 in., Length 9 in.

    b. Width 4 in., Length 9 in.

    c. Width 4 in., Length 5 in.

    d. Width 6 in., Length 11 in.

Pass the COOP!

14. Calculate (3a + 4b) * d when A = 2, b = 4 and d = 8

    a. 40
    b. 150
    c. 112
    d. 176

15. c = 4, n = 5 and x = 3. Calculate 2cnx/2n

    a. 12
    b. 50
    c. 8
    d. 21

16. Simplify 3 1/2 / 2 4/5

    a. 1 1/4
    b. 2 1/4
    c. 1 1/3
    d. 2 1/3

17. Solve 2b/3 + 3a/5 − 2, where b = 9 and a = 10

    a. 5
    b. 10
    c. 20
    d. 9

18. Simplify (1/3 + 2/6) - (3/4 - 1/3)

    a. 1/4
    b. 5/11
    c. 3/7
    d. 2/9

Practice Test Questions Set 2

19. Simplify (4/5 - 3/10) + (2/3 − 3/9) =

    a. 4/11
    b. 5/6
    c. 7/15
    d. 9/11

20. Translate the following into an equation: 2 + a number divided by 7.

    a. (2 + X)/7
    b. (7 + X)/2
    c. (2 + 7)/X
    d. 2/(7 + X)

21. If a = 12 and b = 8, solve 6b - a + 2a

    a. 12/9
    b. 18
    c. 16
    d. 12

22. Simplify 3 2/3 - 1 2/8

    a. 3/5
    b. 3/5
    c. 2 5/12
    d. 1 5/12

23. Simplify 7 2/5 − 4 3/10

    a. 3 1/10
    b. 3 2/5
    c. 4 1/5
    d. 3 7/10

24. Solve for x. -5 – 5x = 8x + 8

    a. 6
    b. 3
    c. 1
    d. 2

25. Solve 2 1/3 x 1 3/7 x 3/4

    a. 2 1/2
    b. 9
    c. 3 2/3
    d. 2 2/5

26. Simplify 7 4/5 – 4 2/3

    a. 4 2/5
    b. 3 2/15
    c. 3 7/15
    d. 4 3/5

27. Solve for x. 12x - 8 = 3x + 10

    a. 6
    b. 4
    c. 2
    d. 3

28. Simplify (3/5 - 2/5) + (3/4 – 2/8)

    a. 18/45
    b. 7/11
    c. 14/20
    d. 12/19

Practice Test Questions Set 2

29. Solve for a. 6a + 4 = 28 + 2a

   a. 4
   b. 8
   c. 2
   d. 6

30. Simplify (3/4 - 1/4) - (3/5 – 2/5)

   a. 9/20
   b. 4/15
   c. 7/15
   d. 11/20

31. Solve for x. 6 + 9x = 12 + 7x

   a. 5
   b. 2
   c. 4
   d. 3

32. Simplify 6 2/5 / 2 2/7

   a. 2 1/4
   b. 1 1/5
   c. 2 4/5
   d. 2 2/3

33. Solve for a. -6 + 7a = 9 + 4a

   a. 3
   b. 5
   c. 2
   d. 6

34. A square lawn has an area of 62,500 square meters. What is the cost of building fence around it at a rate of $5.5 per meter?

    a. $4000
    b. $4500
    c. $5000
    d. $5500

35. The following numbers are the ages of people on a bus – 3, 6, 27, 13, 6, 8, 12, 20, 5, 10. Calculate their average of their ages.

    a. 11
    b. 6
    c. 9
    d. 110

36. A farmer wants to plant 65,536 trees in such a way that number of rows must be equal to the number of plants in a row. How many trees will he plant in a row?

    a. 1684
    b. 1268
    c. 668
    d. 256

37. How much pay does Mr. Johnson receive if he gives half of his pay to his family, $250 to his landlord, and has exactly 3/7 of his pay left after these expenses?

    a. $3600
    b. $3500
    c. $2800
    d. $1750

Practice Test Questions Set 2

38. A boy has 4 red, 5 green and 2 yellow balls. He chooses two balls randomly. What is the probability that one is red and other is green?

    a. 2/11
    b. 19/22
    c. 20/121
    d. 9/11

39. Simplify 5 1/2 – 5 3/7

    a. 1/10
    b. 1/14
    c. 1/7
    d. 2/7

40. What is -3 - (-7) - (+5)?

    a. -6
    b. 6
    c. 3
    d. -1

Answer Key

Section I - Sequences

1. C
There are two letters missing in each sequence.

2. B
The sequence is decreasing. The first two terms decreased by 14 and subsequent differences is decreasing by 2, i.e. 14, 12, 10, 8, 6, 4, 2

3. B
The sequence is increasing by adding 4, 5, 6, 7, 8, 9....etc. The next term is of the sequence is 26 + 7 = 33 and then 33 + 8 = 41

4. C
The pattern alternates two figures and adds a new figure on the end.

5. D
The sequence alternates two instances, then one instance.

6. B
The sequences increases the double-digit 's' each instance.

7. C
The sequence is decreasing by 8.

8. B
The sequence is decreasing by dividing the last term by 2.

9. C
The sequence is increasing by half each time.

10. B
The sequence is increasing by multiplying the last term by 3. 2.7 x 3= 8.1 and 8.1 x 3 = 24.3

Practice Test Questions Set 2

11. C
The sequence is increasing by 9.

12. B
The sequence is decreasing by 5.

13. C
The sequence is decreasing by +5 and -10 alternately. The first term is 75 – 5 = 70 and the last term is 55 + 5 = 60.

14. D
The sequence is increasing by 6.

15. A
The sequence is increasing by 9.

16. D
The sequence is increasing and decreasing alternately. It increases by +5 and decreases by -7. The first term will thus be the second term 95 – 5 = 90 and the last term will be 91 – 7 = 84.

17. B
The difference between the terms starts from 12 and decreases by 2 i.e. 12, 10,8,6,4,2. The missing terms are 46 – 6 = 40 and 34 – 0 = 34.

18. D
Each term is being doubled or multiplied by 2 to get the next term. 3 x 2 = 6 and 12 x 2 = 24.

19. C
The sequence is increasing by 9.

20. C
The difference between the first two terms is 10. The difference between subsequent terms decreases by 1, i.e. 10, 9,8,7,6. Answer is 37 + 6 = 43.

Section II – Analogies

1. B
This is a type relationship. A child is a young human just as a kitten is a young cat.

2. B
This is a composition relationship. A candle is made of wax and a bowl is made of clay.

3. D
This is a part to whole relationship. A petal is to a flower as fur is to a rabbit.

4. A
A present celebrates a birthday and a reward celebrates an accomplishment.

5. C
This is a functional relationship. A shovel is used to dig and scissors are used to snip.

6. A
This is a parts to whole relationship. The finger is part of the hand in the same way that a leg is part of a body.

7. A
This is a cause and effect relationship. If you sleep in you will be late. If you skip breakfast you will be hungry.

8. D
A sphere is the solid form of a circle just as a cube is the solid form of a square.

9. A
This is a classification relationship. An orange is a fruit and a carrot is a vegetable.

10. D
This is a characteristic relationship. Paper is light.

Practice Test Questions Set 2

11. B
This is a composition relationship. Cars are made of steel just as windows are made of glass.

12. A
A product or service of quality is one that adheres to excellence standards and is held free of any damage or deficiencies.

13. D
Fiction is the use of imagination instead of factual statements, and is usually used in prose to create entertaining literary work.

14. C
Desire is a stronger description of a want or wish, which is seen as a longing for something or someone.

15. D
To be responsible means that one holds accountability for one's actions, a situation, or because duty or trust was assigned to them.

16. A
Tendency is the proneness of a particular outcome or a place, event, or effect over another outcome.

17. A
A theory is an attempted explanation created by a set of principles or statements or as a result of a series of situations.

18. A
Expansion is the growth of a space, or spreading out of the number or size of a particular object.

19. A
An approval is a favorable outcome or affirmation; a favorable commendation or opinion, or granting of a permission.

20. C
To measure something means using a scale to measure them against a set of standards.

Section III - Quantitative Reasoning

1. B
8 of the 16 squares are shaded = 1/2.

2. A
Five of the nine squares are shaded corresponding to the fraction 5/9.

3. A
Three of the sex squares are shaded corresponding to the fraction 1/2.

4. C
Two of the nine squares are shaded (1/2 + 1/2 + 1/2 + 1/2) = 2/9.

5. B
Four of the nine squares are shaded (3 + 1/2 + 1/2) corresponding to the fraction 4/9.

6. D
Three of the eight squares are shaded (2 + 1/2 + 1/2) corresponding to the fraction 3/8.

7. A
Six of the twelve squares are shaded corresponding to the fraction 6/12 = 1/2.

8. B
One fleur-de-lis equals 2 cones, so one fleur-de-lis and 2 cones will equal four cones.

9. C
One rectangle equals one star, so 2 rectangles equals one glass and one star.

10. A
Three cones equals three cones.

Practice Test Questions Set 2

11. C
Two diamonds equals one globe, so one diamond and a globe will equal three diamonds.

12. D
The figures are equal and therefore, inter-changeable. If a star equals a hexagon, then one star and one hexagon will equal two stars.

13. A
The number are multiplied by 2.5 each time.

14. C
Seven is subtracted from each number.

15. C
The number related by 2/3. 50 is 2/3 of 75.

16. B
The only certain thing is children enjoy different kinds of sports.

17. B
False Although all students carry a backpack, not everyone who carries a backpack is a student. i.e. there are some people who carry a backpack who are not students.

18. C
The only certain thing is Jane's hobby is reading.

19. D
The only certain thing is bones protect different parts of the body.

20. B False.
There are two problems. Doctors can sometimes predict epidemics. Bird Flu is becoming an epidemic.

Bird flu is not an epidemic yet, and doctors can only predict epidemics sometimes.

21. C Uncertain.
Both the silver and gold fish can swim faster than the black fish, but there is no information how the silver and gold fish swimming against each other.

22. B
False. Just because all dogs are mammals does not mean that all mammals are dogs.

23. A True.
Since all rabbits have fur, and some rabbits are pets, then some pets will have fur.

24. B
False. Based on the first 2 statements you could say that all felines are mammals, but you cannot say that all mammals are felines.

25. B False.
If confers keep their leaves in the fall, the cannot be deciduous.

Section IV – Reading and Language Arts

1. B
We can infer an important part of the respiratory system are the lungs. From the passage, "Molecules of oxygen and carbon dioxide are passively exchanged, by diffusion, between the gaseous external environment and the blood. This process occurs in the alveolar region of the lungs."

Therefore, one primary function for the respiratory system is the exchange of oxygen and carbon dioxide, and this process occurs in the lungs. We can therefore infer that the lungs are an important part of the respiratory system.

2. C
The process by which molecules of oxygen and carbon dioxide are passively exchanged is diffusion.

This is a definition type question. Scan the passage for references to "oxygen," "carbon dioxide," or "exchanged."

Practice Test Questions Set 2

3. A
The organ that plays an important role in gas exchange in amphibians is the skin.

Scan the passage for references to "amphibians," and find the answer.

4. A
The three physiological zones of the respiratory system are Conducting, transitional, respiratory zones.

5. B
When someone is avid about something that means they are highly interested in the subject. The context clues are dull and boring, because they define the opposite of avid.

Choice A is incorrect because dull and boring are not the opposite of good.

Choice C is incorrect because dull and boring are not the opposite of slow.

Choice D is incorrect because you can be a fast reader and still not be interested in what you have read.

6. A
The author is using a simile to compare the books to medicine. Medicine is what you take when you want to feel better. They are suggesting that if a person wants to feel good, they should read Dr. Seuss' books.

Choice B is incorrect because there is no mention of a doctor's office.

Choice C is incorrect because it is using the literal meaning of medicine and the author is using medicine in a figurative way.

Choice D is incorrect because it makes no sense. We know not to eat books.

7. D

The publisher is described as intelligent because he knew to get in touch with a famous author to develop a book that children would be interested in reading.

Choice A is incorrect because we can assume that all book publishers must know how to read.

Choice B is incorrect because it says in the article that more than one publisher was concerned about whether or not children liked to read.

Choice D is incorrect because there is no mention in the article about how well *The Cat in the Hat* sold when it was first published.

8. B

The passage describes in detail how Dr. Seuss had a great effect on the lives of children through his writing. It names several of his books, tells how he helped children become avid readers and explains his style of writing.

Choice A is incorrect because that is just one single fact about the passage.

Choice C is incorrect because that is just one single fact about the passage.

Choice D is incorrect because that is just one single fact about the passage.

Again, choice B is correct because it encompasses ALL the facts in the passage, not just one single fact.

9. B

The first paragraph tells us that myths are a true account of the remote past.

The second paragraph tells us that, "myths generally take place during a primordial age, when the world was still young, before achieving its current form."

Putting these two together, we can infer that humankind used myth to explain how the world was created.

Practice Test Questions Set 2

10. A
This passage is about different types of stories. First, the passage explains myths, and then compares other types of stories to myths.

11. B
Folktales are different to myths, in that, "Unlike myths, folktales can take place at any time and any place, and the natives do not usually consider them true or sacred."

12. B
This passage describes the different categories for traditional stories. The other choices are facts from the passage, not the main idea of the passage. The main idea of a passage will always be the most general statement. For example, choice A, myths, fables, and folktales are not the same thing, and each describes a specific type of story. This is a true statement from the passage, but not the main idea of the passage, since the passage also talks about how some cultures may classify a story as a myth and others as a folktale.

The statement, from choice B, traditional stories can be categorized in different ways by different people, is a more general statement that describes the passage.

13. B
Choice B is the best choice, categories that group traditional stories according to certain characteristics.

Choices A and C are false and can be eliminated right away. Choice D is designed to confuse. Choice D may be true, but it is not mentioned in the passage.

14. D
The best answer is choice D, traditional stories themselves are a part of the larger category of folklore, which may also include costumes, gestures, and music.

All the other choices are false. Traditional stories are part of the larger category of folklore, which includes other things, not the other way around.

15. A
This passage shows there is a distinct difference between a myth and a legend, although, both are folktales.

16. D
"Which" is correct, because the files are objects and not people.

17. C
The simple present tense, "rises," is correct.

18. A
"Lie" does not require a direct object, while "lay" does. The old woman might lie on the couch, which has no direct object, or she might lay the book down, which has the direct object, "the book."

19. D
The simple present tense, "falls," is correct because it is repeated action.

20. A
The present progressive, "building models," is correct in this sentence; it is required to match the other present progressive verbs.

21. A
Past Perfect tense describes a completed action in the past, before another action in the past.

22. B
"Ran well" is correct. "Ran good" is never correct.

23. D
Commas and periods always go inside quotation marks. Question marks that are part of a quote also go inside quotation marks; however, if the writer quotes a statement as part of a larger question, the question mark is placed after the quotation mark.

24. C
The present perfect tense cannot be used with specific time

Practice Test Questions Set 2

expressions such as yesterday, one year ago, last week, when I was a child, at that moment, that day, one day, etc. The present perfect tense is used with unspecific expressions such as ever, never, once, many times, several times, before, so far, already, yet, etc.

25. A
"Went" is used in the simple past tense. "Gone" is used in the past perfect tense.

26. B
"Went" is used in the simple past tense. "Gone" is used in the past perfect tense.

27. D
"It's" is a contraction for it is or it has. "Its" is a possessive pronoun.

28. C
"It's" is a contraction for it is or it has. "Its" is a possessive pronoun.

29. C
The subject in the first phrase, "the boy," has to agree with the subject in the second phrase, "he is."

30. A
These three sentences can be combined using 'although,' and 'since.'

31. A
The word "principal" is a synonym for primary or major. "Principle" means a fundamental truth.

32. D
The article "a" come before a noun that begins with a consonant, while "an" comes before a noun that begins with a vowel.

33. A
"Except" means to exclude something. "Accept" means to receive something, or to agree to an idea.

34. A
"Advise" is a verb that means to offer advice, which is a noun.

35. C
"Adapt" means to change or accommodate. "Adopt" means to accept, embrace, or to assume responsibility or ownership for something or someone.

Section V – Math

1. B
Let XY represent the initial number, X + Y = 12, YX = XY + 36, only b = 48 satisfies both equations.

2. A
The problem is to find the perimeter of a shape made by merging a square and a semi circle. Perimeter = 3 sides of the square + 1/2 circumference of the circle.
= (3 x 5) + ½(5 π)
= 15 + 2.5 π
Perimeter = 17.5 π cm

3. B
Volume = Volume of large cylinder - Volume of small cylinder
(Volume of cylinder = area of base x height)
Volume = (π 12^2 x 10) - (π 6^2 x 5), 1440π - 180π
Volume = 1260π in^3

4. D
We have a circle given with diameter 8 cm and a square located within the circle. We are asked to find the area of the circle for which we only need to know the length of the radius that is the half of the diameter.

Area of circle = $πr^2$ ... r = 8/2 = 4 cm

Area of circle = π * 4^2

= 16π cm^2 ... As we notice, the inner square has no role in this question.

Practice Test Questions Set 2

5. C
In one trip around the track, he covers the distance equal to the circumference of the circular path.
Circumference of the path = 75 × π = 235.65 meters.
Distance covered in 7 times around = 235.65 × 7 = 1650 meters.

6. A
The angles opposite both angles 30° & angle d are respectively equal to vertical angles.
2(30° + d) = 360°
2d = 360° - 60°
2d = 300°
d = 150°

7. C
The length of the track = 1.2 km = 1200 meters.
John will complete 1 round in 1200/120 = 10 minutes.
Tony will complete 1 round in 1200/100 = 12 minutes.
David will complete 1 round in 1200/75 = 16 minutes.
The Least Common Multiple of these is 240. Therefore, they will be together after 240 minutes.

8. D
1 cm = 5 km so 12.4 cm will be = 12.4 × 5 = 62 km.

9. B
Perimeter of a parallelogram is the sum of the sides.

Perimeter = 2(l + b)
Perimeter = 2(3 + 10), 2 x 13
Perimeter = 26 cm

10. D
2009 X 108 is 216,972, or approximately 210,000.

11. D
First, convert everything to seconds.
Song A = 240 + 56 = 296 sec.
Song B = 120 + 30 = 150 sec.
Song C = 600 + 16 = 616 sec.
Total = 296 + 150 + 616 = 1062. Average will be 1062/3 = 354.
In hours, 354/60 = 5 minutes, 54 seconds.

12. B
8.50 * .4 = 3.40 + 1.30 = $4.70

13. B
Formula for perimeter of a rectangle is 2(L + W)
p=26, so 2(L+W) = p

The length is 5 inches more than the width, so
2(w+5) + 2w = 26
2w + 10 + 2w = 26
2w + 2w = 26 - 10
4w = 18
W = 16/4 = 4 inches
L is 5 inches more than w, so
L = 5 + 4 = 9 inches.

14. D
Substitute the known variables, (3 x 2) + (4 x 4) x 8 =, 6 + 16 x 8, 24 x 8 = 176

15. A
2cnx = 2(4 x 5 x 3)/(2 X 5) =
(2 x 60)/(2 x 5) = 120/10 = 12

16. A
First change all the terms to fractions, therefore, we get 7/2 / 14/5, to divide we need to invert the second fraction, 7/2 x 5/14, and then we cancel out to reduce to the lowest terms, 1/2 x 5/2 = 5/4, convert back to proper fraction to get 1 1/4

17. B
Substitute known variables, 2 x 9/3 + 3 x 10/5 – 2 =, 18/3 + 30/5 – 2 =, 6 + 6 -2 =, 12 - 2 = 10

18. A
First solve the fraction in each bracket separately, therefore (1/3 + 2/6) - (3/4 - 1/3) = (find common denominator) (2+2/6) – (9- 4/12) = (4/6) – (5/12) = (find common denominator again) 8/12 – 5/12 =, 8 - 5/12 = 3/12 = 1/4.

Practice Test Questions Set 2

19. B
(4/5 - 3/10) + (2/3 − 3/9) =, (find a common denominator) (8-3/10) + (6-3/9) =, (5/10) + (3/9) = 1/2 + 1/3, (find a common denominator) 3+2/6 = 5/6

20. A
2 + a number divided by 7.
(2 + X) divided by 7.
(2 + X)/7

21. D
Substitute with known variables, (6 x 8) − 12 + (2 x 12) =, 48 − 12 + 24, do the additions first, 48 − (12 + 24) =, 48 − 36 = 12

22. C
Subtract the whole numbers and then subtract the fractions, therefore 3 2/3 - 1 2/8 = (3-1) (2/3 − 2/8) = find common denominator to subtract the fractions, (2) (16-6)/24 = 2 10/24, reduce to lowest terms, 2 5/12

23. A
Subtract the whole numbers and then subtract the fractions, therefore (7-4) (2/5 − 3/10) = 3 (4-3/10) = 3 1/10

24. C
-5 − 5x = 8x + 8, bring same terms to same side of the equation changing the negative or positive signs when they cross over, therefore -5x - 8x = 8 + 5, = -13x = 13, x = 1.

25. A
First, convert all the terms to fractions and then cancel out. Therefore, 7/3 x 10/7 x 3/4 = 1/3 x 10/1 x 3/4, 1 x 5 x 1/2, 5 x 1/2 = 2 1/2

26. B
Subtract the whole numbers and then subtract the fractions, therefore (7 - 4) (4/5 − 2/3) = 3 (12 - 10/15) = 3 2/15

Pass the COOP!

27. C
12x – 8 = 3x + 10, bring same terms to same side of the equation changing the negative or positive signs when they cross over, therefore 12x -3x = 10 + 8, 9x = 18, x = 2

28. C
(3/5 - 2/5) + (3/4 – 2/8) =, (3-2/5) + (6-2/8) =, 1/5 + 4/8 =, (find a common denominator) 8+20/40 = 28/40
= 14/20

29. D
6a + 4 = 28 + 2a, solve for a. Bring same terms to same side of the equation changing the negative or positive signs when they cross over, therefore 6a – 2a = 28 - 4, 4a = 24, a = 24/4 = 6

30. D
(3-1/4) – (3-2/5) =, 3/4 - 1/5 =. 15-4/20 = 11/20

31. D
6 + 9x = 12 + 7x, bring same terms to same side of the equation changing the negative or positive signs when they cross over, therefore 9x – 7x = 12 – 6, 2x = 6, x = 6/2, x = 3

32. C
First change all the terms to fractions, therefore, we get 32/5 / 16/7, to divide we need to invert the second fraction, 32/5 x 7/16, and then we cancel out to reduce to the lowest terms, 2/5 x 7/1 = 14/5, convert back to proper fraction to get 2 4/5

33. B
-6 + 7a = 9 + 4a, bring same terms to same side of the equation changing the negative or positive signs when they cross over, therefore 7a – 4a = 9 + 6 = 3a = 15, a = 15/3, a = 5

34. D
As the lawn is square, the length of one side will be= √62500 = 250 meters. Therefore, the perimeters will be

Practice Test Questions Set 2

250 × 4 = 1000 meters. The total cost will be 1000 × 5.5 = $5500.

35. A
First add all the numbers 3 + 6 + 27 + 13 + 6 + 8 + 12 + 20 + 5 + 10 = 110. Then divide by 10 (the number of data provided) = 110/10 = 11

36. D
Let x be number of rows, and number of trees in a row. So equation becomes $X^2 = 65536$, X = 256.

37. B
We check the fractions in the question and see that there is a "half" (that is 1/2) and 3/7. So, we multiply the denominators of these fractions to decide how to name the total money. We say that Mr. Johnson has 14x at the beginning; he gives half of this, meaning 7x, to his family. $250 to his landlord. He has 3/7 of his money left. 3/7 of 14x is equal to:

14x * (3/7) = 6x

So,

Spent money is: 7x + 250

Unspent money is: 6x

Total money is: 14x

We write an equation: total money = spent money + unspent money

14x = 7x + 250 + 6x

14x - 7x - 6x = 250

x = 250

We are asked to find the total money that is 14x:

14x = 14 * 250 = $3500

38. A
The probability that the 1st ball drawn is red = 4/11. The probability that the 2nd ball drawn is green = 5/10. The combined probability will then be 4/11 X 5/10 = 20/110 = 2/11.

39. B
(5-5) (1/2 – 3/7) = (7-6/14) = 1/14

40. D
-(-) becomes + and -(+) becomes -, therefore, -3 - (-7) - (+5) = -3 + 7 – 5, -4 + 5 = -1

What to Do After Taking a Practice Test

Steps for Maximizing Your Learning and Improvement

Taking a practice test is an excellent way to prepare for any exam, but it's just the beginning of the journey toward mastering the material. The real progress happens after the test when you review, analyze, and learn from your performance. Here are the steps you should take after completing a practice test:

Review Your Answers
Go through each question: Carefully check each question, whether you got it right or wrong. Understanding why you chose a particular answer is crucial to your learning.

Compare with the correct answers: Identify the correct answers and note where your understanding aligns or differs. This can help you pinpoint areas that need more attention.

Understand Your Mistakes
Analyze incorrect answers: For every wrong answer, figure out why it was incorrect. Was it due to a lack of knowledge, a misunderstanding of the question, or a simple mistake? Identify patterns: Look for patterns in your mistakes. Are there specific topics or types of questions where you consistently struggle? Recognizing these patterns is key to targeted improvement.

Revisit the Material
Review related content: Go back to your textbooks, notes, or other study materials to review the topics that you found difficult. This reinforces your understanding and fills in any gaps.

Use additional resources: If needed, seek out additional resources such as online tutorials, videos, or study groups to gain a better grasp of the material.

Practice Similar Questions
Find similar questions: Practice more questions that are similar to the ones you got wrong. This helps solidify your understanding and improve your skills in those areas.

Use varied sources: Utilize different practice tests or question banks to get a wide range of questions and avoid memorizing answers.

Time Management
Assess your timing: Look at how long you took to complete the test and each question. Identify if there were any time sinks and think about how you can manage your time better in the future.

Practice under timed conditions: Simulate exam conditions by practicing under timed constraints. This helps you manage your time effectively and reduces anxiety during the actual test.

Time Management on a Test

https://www.test-preparation.ca/time-management/

Reflect on Your Strategy
Evaluate your approach: Reflect on the strategies you used during the test. Were there specific techniques that worked well or didn't work at all?

Adjust as needed: Based on your reflection, adjust your test-taking strategies. This might include better time management, different approaches to reading questions, or improved methods for eliminating incorrect answers.

Get Feedback
Ask for help: If possible, discuss your practice test with a teacher, tutor, or knowledgeable friend. They can provide valuable insights and explain difficult concepts.

Join study groups: Collaborate with peers who are also preparing for the same exam. Group study can offer new perspectives and shared resources.

Stay Consistent
Regular practice: Make practice tests a regular part of your study routine. Consistent practice helps you track your progress and keep your skills sharp.

Stay motivated: Keep your end goal in mind and remind yourself of the importance of your preparation. Celebrate small victories along the way to stay motivated.

Take Care of Yourself
Rest and recharge: Ensure you get enough rest and relaxation. Overworking can lead to burnout and reduce your effectiveness in studying.

Maintain a healthy lifestyle: Eat well, exercise regularly, and stay hydrated. A healthy body supports a sharp mind.

Super Foods for Studying
https://test-preparation.ca/super-foods-studying/

By following these steps, you'll not only improve your performance on practice tests but also enhance your overall understanding and confidence. Remember, practice tests are a tool for learning, not just assessment. Use them wisely, and you'll see significant progress on your path to success.

Conclusion

CONGRATULATIONS! You have made it this far because you have applied yourself diligently to practicing for the exam and no doubt improved your potential score considerably! Getting into a good school is a huge step in a journey that might be challenging at times but will be many times more rewarding and fulfilling. That is why being prepared is so important.

Study then Practice and then Succeed!

Good Luck!

Register for Free Updates and More Practice Test Questions

Register your purchase at

https://www.test-preparation.ca/register/ for fast and convenient access to updates, errata, free test tips and more practice test questions.

ONLINE RESOURCES

How to Prepare for a Test - The Ultimate Guide

https://www.test-preparation.ca/prepare-test/

Learning Styles - The Complete Guide

https://www.test-preparation.ca/learning-style/

Test Anxiety Secrets!

https://www.test-preparation.ca/test-anxiety/

Time Management on a Test

https://www.test-preparation.ca/time-management/

Flash Cards - The Complete Guide

https://www.test-preparation.ca/flash-cards/

How to Memorize - The Complete Guide

https://www.test-preparation.ca/memorize/

Super Foods for Studying

https://test-preparation.ca/super-foods-studying/

www.ingramcontent.com/pod-product-compliance
Lightning Source LLC
Chambersburg PA
CBHW071953070526
44583CB00015B/1169